MODERN

TURKISH

A COMPLETE SELF-STUDY COURSE FOR BEGINNERS

COMPREHENSIVE

THE MOST UP TO DATE GRAMMAR RULES

FOR LEARNERS ELEMENTARY TO UPPER INTERMEDIATE

AN IDEAL SYSTEM FOR ADULTS WITH LIMITED LEARNING TIME

B. ORHAN DOĞAN

Modern Turkish   Copyright © Bekir Orhan Doğan

ISBN   975-94219-0-9

First published :   March 1999
Second edition :   May 2003
Third edition   :   April 2005

Distributed by:

BORA YAYINCILIK
Halkalı Toplu Konutları (ATAKENT), 2. Etap, C 510/4
Halkalı – İstanbul
Tel : (0212) 470 04 38 – (0532) 381 92 36
Fax : (0212) 470 04 38
www.borayayincilik.com
www.ingilizcem.com
E-mail: myenglish@ingilizcem.com - ordogan@hotmail.com

BEŞİR KİTABEVİ
Sahaflar Çarşısı, No: 28   Beyazıt- İstanbul
Tel-Fax: +90 212 512 60 07

Printed in Turkey by
MART Matbaacılık Sanatları Ticaret ve Sanayi Ltd. Şti. , İstanbul
Mart Plaza, Merkez mah. Ceylan sok. 24   Nurtepe / Kağıthane – İst.
www.martmatbaa.com.tr
martgrafik@superonline.com
bektas@martmatbaa.com.tr

TABLE OF CONTENTS

INTRODUCTION

This book is designed for English-speaking students of any age who set out to learn modern Turkish for social, business and casual purposes in an adult environment.

It aims to give you a solid foundation on which to build, so that you can recognize, understand, and begin to use the basic patterns of modern standard Turkish.

All the basic grammar used in modern Turkish is presented clearly and comprehensively.

Hundreds of helpful examples and exercises are covered.

You will also be helped by 'the key to exercises' and the accompanying CD.

LESSON 1

♦ THE ALPHABET

There are 29 letters in the Turkish Alphabet.

LETTER	NAME	PRONUNCIATION
A a	a	as **u** in **run**
B b	be	as in English
C c	ce	as **g** in **giant**
Ç ç	çe	as **ch** in **change**
D d	de	as in English
E e	e	as in **get**
F f	fe	as in English
G g	ge	as in **get**
Ğ ğ	yumuşak g (soft g) (**)	
H h	he	as in **hotel**
I ı	ı	as the third vowel in **enjoyable**
İ i	i	as in **fit**
J j	je	as **s** in **measure**
K k	ke	as in **kitchen**
L l	le	as in English
M m	me	as in English
N n	ne	as in English
O o	o	as in **novel**
Ö ö	ö	as 'ö' in German **österreich**
P p	pe	as in English

R	r	re	as in **rabbit**
S	s	se	as in **sad**
Ş	ş	şe	as **sh** in **shade**
T	t	te	as in English
U	u	u	as in **pull**
Ü	ü	ü	as **'ü'** in German **übung**
V	v	ve	as in English
Y	y	ye	as in **yes**
Z	z	ze	as in English

■ Note that **Q, W** and **X** do not occur in the Turkish alphabet.

■ Turkish spelling is phonetic. The same letter always indicates the same sound.

■ The English Alphabet does not have the following letters which the Turkish Alphabet contains:

Ç ç	I ı (the undotted i) (*)
Ğ ğ	Ö ö
Ş ş	Ü ü

(*) The capital form of ' **I** ' is ' **I** '

The capital form of ' **i** ' is ' **İ** ' (the dotted **i**).

....

✿ EXERCISE 1

Look at the list of the letters in the alphabet and listen to your CD. Repeat the letters in the gaps provided. If you are not satisfied with your attempt, try again.

....

(**) SOFT G (Yumuşak g)

The 'yumuşak g' never begins a word. When it is preceded and followed by 'e, i, ö or ü', it sounds like English 'y', as in **eğer** (if). Otherwise it indicates that the preceding vowel is lengthened, as in **dağ** (mountain).

 ## EXERCISE 2

Look at the following words. Listen to your CD carefully and try to see what happens when the 'yumuşak g' occurs. Repeat the words in the gaps provided.

1. **ağır**   heavy, slow
2. **ağlamak**   crying, to cry
3. **buğday**   wheat, corn
4. **doğum**   birth
5. **değirmen**   mill
6. **diğer**   other
7. **düğün**   feast

THE CIRCUMFLEX ACCENT (^)

- ■ This accent may stand over the vowels '**a, ı** and **u**'.
- ■ When it stands over the letter '**a**' which is preceded by **g, k** or **l**, the circumflex accent indicates that the preceding consonant is followed by a short '**y**' sound.

- • **Lâtin**   Latin
- • **kârlı**   profitable
- • **kanaatkâr**   contented, abstinent
- • **lâmba**   lamp
- • **dükkân**   shop, shebang

■ Elsewhere the circumflex indicates that the vowel it stands over is
to be prolonged.

- **âciz**   weak, incapable
- **dâhil**   included, inclusive
- **millî**   national
- **ilmî**   scientific
- **ebedî**   everlasting

■ The words in which the circumflex occurs are originally Arabic.

EXERCISE 3

Look at the following words. Listen carefully to your CD and see
what happens when the circumflex occurs. Repeat the words in the
gaps provided.

1. kârlı	6. dâhil
2. kanaatkâr	7. dâhi
3. lâmba	8. ilmî
4. dükkân	9. ebedî
5. âciz	10. millî

■ Occasionally 'a' sound is prolonged in some words (originally
Arabic) which have 'a' in their first syllable.

EXERCISE 4

Look at the words in the following list and listen to your CD.

1. **galip**	victorious	5. **amir**	chief, commanding
2. **katil**	murderer	6. **adil**	fair
3. **hamile**	pregnant	7. **salim**	safe
4. **cahil**	ignorant	8. **zalim**	cruel

♦ SYLLABIFICATION

Turkish have six syllable patterns. Each syllable begins with a single consonant or a single vowel.

Examples:

- **genç**   young
- **alt**   bottom
- **sen**   you
- **el**   hand
- **ne**   what
- **o**   he, she, it, that (demonstrative)

Stress

In Turkish words the stress is variable and depends on the position of the word in the sentence. It normally falls on the last syllable except in place-names and adverbs. In compound words the stress falls on the last syllable of the first element.

....

 EXERCISE 5

Look at the following words and listen to your CD. Repeat the
words in the gaps provided :

1.	**güzel**	pretty, beautiful	28.	**ağız**	mouth
2.	**çirkin**	ugly	29.	**kulak**	ear
3.	**genç**	young	30.	**kol**	arm
4.	**yaşlı**	old	31.	**el**	hand
5.	**büyük**	big, large	32.	**büyükanne**	grandmother
6.	**küçük**	small, little	33.	**büyükbaba**	grandfather
7.	**pahalı**	expensive	34.	**şehir**	city
8.	**ucuz**	cheap	35.	**il**	city
9.	**temiz**	clean	36.	**kent**	city
10.	**pis**	dirty	37.	**kasaba**	town
11.	**dolu**	full	38.	**köy**	village
12.	**boş**	empty	39.	**cadde**	street. avenue
13.	**sıcak**	hot	40.	**sokak**	road
14.	**soğuk**	cold	41.	**okul**	school
15.	**uzun**	long, tall	42.	**ev**	house
16.	**kısa**	short, brief	43.	**ve**	and
17.	**alt**	bottom	44.	**ile**	with
18.	**üst**	top	45.	**su**	water
19.	**çocuk**	child	46.	**çay**	tea
20.	**oğul**	son	47.	**kahve**	coffee
21.	**kız**	daughter, girl	48.	**süt**	milk
22.	**anne**	mother	49.	**peynir**	cheese
23.	**baba**	father	50.	**şeker**	sugar
24.	**baş**	head	51.	**tereyağı**	butter
25.	**diş**	tooth	52.	**meyve**	fruit
26.	**yüz**	face	53.	**tunç**	bronze
27.	**göz**	eye	54.	**harç**	mortar

....

LESSON 2

♦ SUBJECT PRONOUNS

ben	I
sen	you (informal, familiar singular)
o	he, she, it
biz	we
siz	you (formal, polite singular and plural)
onlar	they

♦ INTERROGATIVES

nasıl?	how?,
ne?	what?
kim?	who?
kaç?	how many?, how much?
ne zaman?	when?, what time?
nerede?	where?
nereye?	where?, to what place?
hangi?	which?

♦ DEMONSTRATIVES

bu	this
bunlar	these
şu	that
şunlar	those
o	that
onlar	those

♦ TURKISH NAMES

♦ For the names of men, **'Bay'** or **'Bey'** indicates English **'Mr.'**

Bay (Atakan) Demir   (or) after the first name: **Atakan Bey**
Mr. (Atakan) Demir   Mr. (Atakan) Demir

♦ For the names of women **'Bayan'** or **'Hanım'** indicates
either **'Mrs'** or **'Miss'**:

Bayan Pınar Demir   (or) after the first name: **Pınar Hanım**
Mrs (Miss) (Pınar) Demir   Mrs (Miss) (Pınar) Demir

♦ NUMBERS

bir	1	yirmi iki	22
iki	2	yirmi üç	23
üç	3	yirmi dört	24
dört	4	yirmi beş	25
beş	5	yirmi altı	26
altı	6	otuz	30
yedi	7	kırk	40
sekiz	8	elli	50
dokuz	9	altmış	60
on	10	yetmiş	70
on bir	11	seksen	80
on iki	12	doksan	90
on üç	13	doksan dokuz	99
on dört	14	yüz	100
on beş	15	iki yüz	200
on altı	16	bin	1 000
on yedi	17	iki bin	2 000
on sekiz	18	on bin	10 000
on dokuz	19	yirmi bin	20 000
yirmi	20	yüz bin	100 000
yirmi bir	21	iki yüz bin	200 000
		(bir)milyon	1 000 000
		(bir)milyar	1 000 000 000

bir araba	one car, a car
iki araba	two cars, the two cars
bir adam	one man, a man
iki adam	two men, the two men
bir kez	one time, once
bir kere	one time, once
bir defa	one time, once
iki kez	two times, twice

■ **'Yarım'** is the word for 'one half'. It is used when there is no other number in the expression.

- **yarım saat**   1/2 hour
- **yarım kilo**   1/2 kilogram
- **yarım elma**   1/2 apple

■ **Buçuk** is used with numerals.

- bir **buçuk** kilo   1 1/2   kilograms
- iki **buçuk** saat   2 1/2   hours

BİRİNCİ, İKİNCİ,.....(first, second,...)

- **birinci**   first
- **ikinci**   second
- **üçüncü**   third
- **dördüncü**   fourth
- **beşinci**   fifth
- **altıncı**   sixth
- **yedinci**   seventh
- **sekizinci**   eighth
- **dokuzuncu**   ninth
- **onuncu**   tenth

BİRER, İKİŞER,... (Distributive Form of Numbers)

birer	yirmişer
ikişer	otuzar
üçer	kırkar
dörder	ellişer
beşer	altmışar
altışar	yetmişer
yedişer	seksener
sekizer	doksanar
dokuzar	yüzer
onar	biner

■ They are usually said twice : **birer birer**   one by one

 EXERCISE 6

Look at the following list of the numbers and listen to your CD.
Repeat the numbers in the gaps provided.

1	10	19	28	37	100	109	190
2	11	20	29	38	101	110	200
3	12	21	30	39	102	120	300
4	13	22	31	40	103	130	400
5	14	23	32	50	104	140	500
6	15	24	33	60	105	150	1000
7	16	25	34	70	106	160	1001
8	17	26	35	80	107	170	1002
9	18	27	36	90	108	180	2000

3000	100 000	1 000 000
4000	200 000	1 000 000 000
5000	500 000	
10 000	900 000	
20 000	999 000	

Birinci, ikinci, üçüncü, dördüncü, beşinci, altıncı, yedinci, sekizinci,
dokuzuncu, onuncu

1/2 (yarım) ekmek , 2 1/2 (iki buçuk) kilo portakal , bir araba, bir
adam, iki adam, iki araba , bir kez , iki kez, bir kere , iki kere , bir
defa , iki defa

◆ Ne kadar , Kaç tane, Birkaç , Biraz , Birçok
(How much, how many, a few,   a little, lots of)

■ The counting word '**Kaç**' is used to mean 'how many' and 'how much'.

• **ne kadar?**	how much?
• **kaç tane?**	how many?
• **kaç para?**	how much money?
• **kaç dolar?**	how many dollars?
• **kaç lira?**	how many liras?
• **çok**	much, many, lots of
• **az**	little, few
• **çok az**	very little
• **biraz**	a little
• **birkaç**	few, a few
• **çok fazla**	too much, too many
• **birçok**	lots of , a lot of, plenty of
• **para**	money
• **çok para**	much money, lots of money
• **az para**	little money
• **çok az para**	very little money
• **çok fazla para**	too much money
• **bir elma**	one apple, an apple
• **birkaç elma**	a few apples
• **çok elma**	many apples
• **birçok elma**	a lot of apples
• **çok fazla elma**	too many apples
• **şeker**	sugar
• **az şeker**	little sugar
• **biraz şeker**	a little sugar
• **çok az şeker**	very little sugar
• **çok fazla şeker**	too much sugar

☛ Note that the above counting words are followed by singular nouns.

■ Countable nouns may be preceded by the countable word '**tane**'

- **kaç elma?**   how many apples?
- **kaç tane elma?**   how many apples?
- **altı sandalye (*)**   six chairs
- **altı tane sandalye**   six chairs
- **beş(tane) kitap (**)**   five books

(*) Note that numbers are followed by singular nouns.
(**) The word '**tane**' may be omitted.

 ## EXERCISE 7

A) Listen to your CD and repeat the words in the gaps provided.

1. ne kadar?	10. birkaç elma	19. çok fazla şeker
2. kaç para?	11. çok elma	20. kaç elma?
3. kaç dolar?	12. birçok elma	21. kaç tane elma?
4. para	13. çok fazla elma	22. altı sandalye
5. çok para	14. şeker	23. altı tane sandalye
6. az para	15. az şeker	24. beş kitap
7. çok az para	16. biraz şeker	25. beş tane kitap
8. çok fazla para	17. çok az şeker	26. Kaç tane kitap?
9. bir elma	18. çok şeker	

B)Try to write in Turkish. Then listen to your CD and check your answers.

1. five kilos of sugar
2. sixty grams
3. sixty-five and a half grams
4. one half kilo of sugar
5. 365 days
6. 52 weeks
7. 12 months
8. 999
9. 10 years
10. how much sugar?
11. how many apples?
12. a little milk
13. a lot of chairs
14. a few tables
15. little water
16. many trees
17. too many students
18. too much meat
19. how many oranges?
20. very little tea
21. seven books
22. a few books
23. much money

◆TIMES AND SEASONS

Days of The Week

Pazartesi	Monday
Salı	Tuesday
Çarşamba	Wednesday
Perşembe	Thursday
Cuma	Friday
Cumartesi	Saturday
Pazar	Sunday

Pazartesi **günü** (*)	**on** Monday
Salı **günü**	**on** Tuesday
Çarşamba **günü**	**on** Wednesday
....	

(*) The word **günü** may be omitted.

Months of the Year and Seasons

Ocak	January	Temmuz	July
Şubat	February	Ağustos	August
Mart	March	Eylül	September
Nisan	April	Ekim	October
Mayıs	May	Kasım	November
Haziran	June	Aralık	December

Kış	İlkbahar	Yaz	Sonbahar
Winter	Spring	Summer	Autumn

◆ Meeting somebody, Greetings, Thanks, Excuses

- Merhaba!
- Merhaba!

- **Merhaba!**   Hello!
- **Selam!**   Hi !
- **Günaydın**   Good morning
- **İyi günler**   Have a good day / Good afternoon
- **Tünaydın (İyi günler)**   Good afternoon
- **İyi akşamlar**   Good evening
- **İyi geceler**   Good night
- **Ne haber?**   How is life?
- **Nasılsınız?**   How are you?
- **İyi, teşekkürler.Ya siz?**   Fine, thanks. And you?
- **İyi şanslar**   Good luck

- **Sonra görüşürüz / Görüşmek üzere**   See you later
- **Allahaısmarladık / Hoşça kalın** (by the one who is leaving)   Goodbye.
- **Güle güle** (by the one who remains)   Goodbye.
- **(Çok) Teşekkür ederim**   Thank you (very much)
- **Bir şey değil**   That's all right / You're welcome
- **Affedersiniz**   Excuse me
- **Özür dilerim**   I beg your pardon

-Affedersiniz ! (Özür dilerim!)

- **Sizi tanıştırayım**   Let me introduce you
- **Bay / Bayan ……..**   This is Mr/Mrs. ………
- **Memnun oldum**   How do you do ?
- **Tanıştığımıza sevindim**   Pleased to meet you

- Tanıştırayım.
  Annem, Aslı.

♦ Kaç Yaşındasınız? - How old are you?

(Ben)	Kaç **yaşında**yım?	How old am I?
(Sen)	Kaç **yaşında**sın?	How old are you?
(O)	Kaç **yaşında**?	How old is he/she/it?
(Biz)	Kaç **yaşında**yız?	How old are we?
(Siz)	Kaç **yaşında**sınız?	How old are you?
(Onlar)	Kaç **yaşında**(lar)?	How old are they?

(Ben)	Otuz **yaşında**yım.	I'm thirty years old.
(Sen)	Otuz **yaşında**sın.	You're thirty years old.
(O)	Otuz **yaşında**.	He's thirty years old.
(Biz)	Otuz **yaşında**yız.	We're thirty years old.
(Siz)	Otuz **yaşında**sınız.	You're thirty years old.
(Onlar)	Otuz **yaşında**(lar).	They're thirty years old.

EXERCISE 8

Look at the following list and listen to your CD. Repeat in the gaps provided.

1. Pazartesi	13. Haziran	25. Günaydın!
2. Salı	14. Temmuz	26. İyi günler!
3. Çarşamba	15. Ağustos	27. Tünaydın!
4. Perşembe	16. Eylül	28. İyi akşamlar!
5. Cuma	17. Ekim	29. İyi geceler!
6. Cumartesi	18. Kasım	30. Nasılsınız?
7. Pazar	19. Aralık	31. Görüşmek üzere!
8. Ocak	20. Kış	32. Allahaısmarladık!
9. Şubat	21. İlkbahar	33. Hoşça kalın!
10. Mart	22. Yaz	34. Güle güle!
11. Nisan	23. Sonbahar	35. Teşekkür ederim
12. Mayıs	24. Merhaba!	36. Bir şey değil

LESSON 3

♦VOWEL HARMONY RULE

There are two groups of vowels in the Turkish Alphabet :

A) a , ı , o , u

B) e , i , ö , ü

♦ The vowels in the group **A** are called **back vowels**. They are formed toward the back of the mouth.

♦ The vowels in the group **B** are called **front vowels**. They are formed in front of the mouth.

Vowel Harmony Rule :

All the vowels in the original Turkish words tend to be in the same group.

The final vowel of the word is called 'dominant vowel'. The group of the final vowel in the word determines the group of the vowel in the suffix. If another suffix is to be added to the first suffix, the vowel in the first suffix becomes the dominant vowel.

Study the following examples and try to understand how the harmony rule works.

- **güzeldir** ...... is pretty, beautiful
- **yaşlıdır** ...... is old
- **uzundur** ...... is tall, long
- **üzgündür** ...... is sad, worried

♦ ADJECTIVES AND INDEFINITE ARTICLE

Adjective + noun is used as in English. The adjective modifies the noun it precedes.

- **güzel kız** (the) pretty girl
- **genç kadın** (the) young woman
- **ilginç kitap** (the) interesting book
- **uzun (boylu) çocuk** (the) tall child
- **kısa (boylu) adam** (the) short man

☛ Note that there is no definite article (the) in Turkish. Any noun may be understood with or without 'the'.

■ The English indefinite article(a, an) is expressed in Turkish by **bir**. The word **bir** serves as the indefinite article and as the number 'one'.

- **bir adam** a man, one man
- **bir köpek** a dog, one dog
- **bir çocuk** a child, one child
- **bir limon** a lemon, one lemon
- **bir bardak su** a glass of water, one glass of water

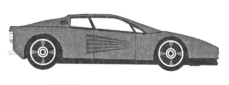

Bu bir araba(dır)

Bu bir çiçek(tir)

Bu bir anahtardır

Bu bir aslandır

Bu bir büyüteçtir

Bu bir güvercindir

Bu bir kaplumbağadır

Bu bir aslan **değildir**

♦ When the indefinite article and adjective(s) modify one noun, the indefinite article is followed by the noun.

- **Güzel bir kız**   A pretty girl
- **Çok uzun bir çocuk**   A very tall child
- **Genç, güzel bir kız**   A young, pretty girl
- **Ne güzel bir kız !**   What a pretty girl !

♦In the following sentences the adjectives preceded by the nouns are used as predicate adjectives. The suffix **'dır/dir/dur/dür'** which is the third person form (present tense) of **'to be:** olmak' may be omitted. It is normally used in the formal written language.

- **Bu kız güzel(dir).**   This girl is pretty.
- **Bu çocuk üzgün(dür).**   This child is sad.
- **Bu iyi(dir).**   This is good.
- **Bu kadın yaşlı(dır).**   This woman is old.
- **Bu ev yeni(dir), diğer ev eski(dir).**
                        This house is new, the other house is old.
- **Bu adam uzun boylu(dur).**   This man is tall.

♦ You can use the word **'değil**: not' to make the above sentences negative.

- Bu kız güzel **değil**(dir).   This girl is **not** pretty.
- Bu iyi **değil**(dir).   This is **not** good.
- Bu adam genç **değil**(dir).   This man is **not** young.
- Bu ev yeni **değil**(dir).   This house is **not** new.

Ne güzel bir kız !

■ **'mı / mi / mu / mü'** is the interrogative particle. It is written as an independent word.

• ..... güzel **mi** (dir)**?**	is ..... pretty?
• ..... akıllı **mı** (dır)**?**	is ..... intelligent?
• ..... büyük **mü** (dür)**?**	is ..... big?
• ..... ucuz **mu** (dur)**?**	is ..... cheap?
• ..... güzel **değil mi?**	isn't .... pretty?
• ..... akıllı **değil mi?**	isn't .... intelligent?
• ..... büyük **değil mi?**	isn't .... big?
• ..... ucuz **değil mi?**	isn't .... cheap?

Question Tag

'değil mi?' is also used as an equivalent to 'question tags'.

- **O pahalı(dır), değil mi?**
  It is expensive, isn't it?
- **Onlar ucuz(dur) , değil mi?**
  They are cheap, aren't they?
- **O bir doktor(dur), değil mi?**
  She/he is a doctor, isn't she(he)?

EXERCISE 9

Look at the following list and listen to your CD Repeat the words in the gaps provided.

1. Güzel bir kız
2. Bir dilim ekmek
3. İlginç bir kitap
4. Bir bardak su
5. Genç, güzel bir kız
6. Bu ev yenidir, diğer ev eskidir
7. Bu kız güzel değil
8. Bu ev yeni değil

9. Bu kız güzel mi?
10. Bu adam akıllı mı?
11. Bu kız güzel değil mi?
12. Bu kız güzel, değil mi?
13. O ev büyük mü?
14. O ev büyük değil mi?
15. O ev büyük, değil mi?

◆ EMPHATICS

There are special emphatic forms of many adjectives. You can find them in dictionaries as separate words. The stress falls on the first syllable.

- **kara**   black
- **kap**kara   black as can be

- **siyah**   black
- **sim**siyah   black as can be

- **beyaz**   white
- **bem**beyaz   white as can be

- **pembe**   pink
- **pes**pembe   pink as can be

- **kırmızı**   red
- **kıp**kırmızı   red as can be

- **mavi**   blue
- **mas**mavi   blue as can be

- **mor**   purple
- **mos**mor   purple as can be

- **yeşil**   green
- **yem**yeşil   green as can be

- **çıplak**   naked
- **çır**(ıl)çıplak stark naked

- **uzun**   long
- **up**uzun   extremely long

◆ THE PLURAL

The plural is formed by adding the suffix **'ler/lar'** to the singular.

After **e, i, ö, ü** in the last syllable :	**-ler**
After **a, ı, o, u** in the last syllable :	**-lar**

- **çocuk**   (the) child
- çocuk**lar**   (the) children

- **defter**   (the) notebook
- defter**ler**   (the) notebooks

- **masa**   (the) table
- masa**lar**   (the) tables

- **etek**   (the) skirt
- etek**ler**   (the) skirts

- **dağ**   (the) mountain
- dağ**lar**   (the) mountains

- **gün**   (the) day
- gün**ler**   (the) days

Bazı (some)

Bazı is the word for English 'some'. It is followed by a noun with a plural suffix.

- **bazı kızlar**   some girls
- **bazı günler**   some days
- **bazı çocuklar**   some children
- **bazı zamanlar**   sometimes
- **bazı dağlar**   some mountains
- **bazı göller**   some lakes

■ When a noun is preceded by a number, the plural suffix is not used.

- adam   adamlar   iki adam
- kadın   kadınlar   beş kadın
- kız   kızlar   yedi kız
- çocuk   çocuklar   dokuz çocuk

....

 EXERCISE 10

Look at the following list and listen to your CD. Repeat in the gaps provided.

1. defter
2. defterler
3. masa
4. masalar
5. etek
6. etekler
7. dağ
8. dağlar
9. gün
10. günler
11. bazı kızlar
12. bazı günler
13. bazı çocuklar
14. bazı zamanlar
15. bazı dağlar
16. bazı göller
17. adam
18. adamlar
19. iki adam
20. kadın
21. kadınlar
22. beş kadın
23. kız
24. kızlar
25. yedi kız
26. çocuk
27. çocuklar
28. dokuz çocuk

....

♦ CHANGES IN CONSONANTS

There are two groups of consonants in the Turkish Alphabet:

A) Voiceless consonants : **ç, f, h, k, p, s, ş, t**
B) Voiced consonants   :   All other consonants.

■ The voiceless consonants '**ç, k, p** and **t**' may be replaced by their voiced counterparts '**c, ğ, b** and **d**'. We can show them by following symbols:

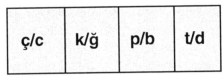

ç/c	k/ğ	p/b	t/d

■ Two sorts of consonant change may occur:

1) The initial consonant of the suffix may be changed.

When the suffix begins with the variable consonant '**t/d** or **ç/c**' :

a. If the suffix is attached to a voiced consonant, the first variable consonant appears as '**d**' or '**c**'.

- **cam**   glass
- camc**ı**   glass-seller
- **çay**   tea
- çayc**ı**   tea-maker, tea-seller
- **güzel**   pretty
- güzel**dir**   ... is pretty
- **uzun**   tall
- uzun**dur**   ... is tall
- **kalın**   thick
- kalın**dır**   ... is thick

b. If the suffix is attached to a voiceless consonant, the initial consonant of the suffix appears as '**ç**' or '**t**'.

- **süt**   milk
- sütçü   milkman
- **aş**   cooked food
- aşçı   cook
- **balık**   fish
- balıkçı   fisherman
- **büyük**   big(huge, large)
- büyüktür   ... is big(huge, large)
- **küçük**   small(little)
- küçüktür   ... is small(little)
- **genç**   young
- gençtir   ....is young

2) Final consonant of preceding word may be changed.

When the final letter is a voiceless variable consonant, it remains unchanged unless it is followed by a suffixed vowel.

• balı**k**	balıkçı	balı**ğ**ı
(the) fish	(the) fisherman	the fish (objective definite)
• koltu**k**	koltukta	koltu**ğ**u
(the) armchair	in the armchair	the armchair (obj. def.)
• ağa**ç**	ağaçta	ağa**c**ı
(the) tree	in the tree	the tree (obj. def.)

EXERCISE 11

Look at the following list and listen to your CD. Repeat the words in the gaps provided.

1. cam   - camcı
2. çay   - çaycı
3. güzel - güzeldir
4. uzun - uzundur

5. kalın - kalındır
6. süt   - sütçü
7. aş   - aşçı
8. balık - balıkçı
9. büyük - büyüktür
10. küçük - küçüktür
11. genç - gençtir
12. balık - balıkçı - balığı
13. koltuk - koltukta - koltuğu

....

Bora bir futbolcudur

Ayşe bir tenisçidir

LESSON 4

♦ SUFFIXES

The most essential characteristic of Turkish is its use of suffixes. Where English uses separate words and prefixes, Turkish expresses the sense by means of suffixes. Turkish does not use prefixes except for a few words borrowed from other languages. A suffix is often added to a Turkish word in order to convey the meaning.

The suffixes '...lı/li/lu/lü' and '...sız/siz/suz/süz'

■ The suffix '...lı / li / lu / lü' is used to form adjectives meaning 'possessed of', 'having'.

• **akıl**	intelligence	akıl**lı**	intelligent
• **ev**	house	ev**li**	married
• **tuz**	salt	tuz**lu**	salty
• **örtü**	cover	örtü**lü**	covered
• **umut**	hope	umut**lu**	hopeful

■ The suffix '...sız / siz / suz / süz' is used to form adjectives meaning 'without', '-less'.

• akıl**lı**	intelligent	akıl**sız**	unreasonable, foolish
• umut**lu**	hopeful	umut**suz**	hopeless
• dikkat**li**	careful	dikkat**siz**	careless
• renk**li**	colourful	renk**siz**	colourless
• mut**lu**	happy	mut**suz**	unhappy
• toz**lu**	dusty	toz**suz**	dustless
• başarı**lı**	successful	başarı**sız**	unsuccessful
• güç**lü**	powerful	güç**süz**	powerless
• akıl**lı**	intelligent	akıl**sız**	stupid

The suffix '...lık/lik/luk/lük'

This suffix is used to form abstract nouns or the name of the profession. It usually means **'-ness'**.

- **güzel**   beautiful
- güzel**lik**   beauty

- **bankacı**   banker
- bankacı**lık**   banking

- **parasız**   moneyless
- parasız**lık**   destitution, poverty

- **akıllı**   clever, intelligent
- akıllı**lık**   wisdom, intelligence

- **büyük**   great, large
- büyük**lük**   greatness, size

- **gazeteci**   journalist
- gazeteci**lik**   journalism

- **küçük**   small
- küçük**lük**   smallness

- **suçlu**   guilty
- suçlu**luk**   guiltiness

- **suçsuz**   innocent
- suçsuz**luk**   innocence

- **ucuz**   cheap
- ucuz**luk**   cheapness

The suffix '...c(ç)ı / c(ç)i / c(ç)u / c(ç)ü'

Nouns formed by using this suffix indicates the person who does the profession.

• **kitap**	book	kitap**çı**	bookseller
• **futbol**	football	futbol**cu**	footballer
• **tamir**	repair	tamir**ci**	repairman
• **odun**	firewood	odun**cu**	seller of firewood
• **sanat**	art	sanat**çı**	artisan
• **süt**	milk	süt**çü**	milkman

The suffix '...c(ç)ık / c(ç)ik / c(ç)uk / c(ç)ük'

This suffix is used after noun to form diminutive. It indicates smallness, affection, sarcasm or contempt.

• **kitap**	book
• kitap**çık**	little book
• **ada**	island
• ada**cık**	little island, isle
• **Ali**	
• Ali**cik**	little Ali, good old Ali

■ A final '**k**' may drop out before the suffix.

• **mini**k	tiny
• mini**cik**	very tiny
• **ufa**k	little
• ufa**cık**	tiny

■ The suffix '...c(ç)ağız / c(ç)eğiz' is used pityingly.

• **adam**	man
• adam**cağız**	poor man

EXERCISE 12

Look at the following list and listen to your CD. Repeat the words in the gaps provided.

1. akıl - akıllı - akılsız
2. ev - evli -evsiz
3. tuz - tuzlu - tuzsuz
4. akıllı - akıllılık
5. güzel - güzellik
6. kitap - kitapçı
7. futbol - futbolcu
8. kitap - kitapçık
9. ada - adacık
10. minik - minicik
11. adam - adamcağız

Zavallı adamcağız!

♦ VERBS

The infinitive is formed by adding the suffix '**mek / mak**' to the simple verb(verb stem) which is the singular imperative.

The infinitive is the verb form in the Turkish dictionaries. In this form the final syllable of the verb appears as '**mek**' or '**mak**'.

Infinitive		Verb stem	
gelmek	coming, to come	**gel**	come
gitmek	going, to go	**git**	go
oturmak	sitting, to sit	**otur**	sit
olmak	being, to be	**ol**	be
okumak	reading, to read	**oku**	read
yazmak	writing, to write	**yaz**	write
bakmak	looking, to look	**bak**	look
gülmek	laughing, to laugh	**gül**	laugh

Negative Form

A verb is turned into the negative by attaching the negative sign **'me/ma'** directly to the verb stem. In the negative form the stress falls on the first syllable of the word.

gitmemek	not going, not to go
gitme !	don't go !

Verb Stem + '(y)ış / (y)iş / (y)uş / (y)üş'

forms the noun of manner.

- **yürü**mek — to walk
- yürü**yüş** — (way of) walking

- **bak**mak — to look
- bak**ış** — (way of) looking (after)

- **ara**mak — to search, to investigate
- ara**yış** — (way of) searching, (way) of investigating,

Verb Stem + ' ıcı / ici / ucu / ücü '

indicates the person who performs the action involved.

- **yüzmek** to swim — yüz**ücü** swimmer
- **koşmak** to run — koş**ucu** runner
- **satmak** to sell — sat**ıcı** seller
- **almak** to buy, to receive — al**ıcı** buyer, receiver

Gidelim - Let's go

yap**ayım**	let me do / let me make
yap**sın**	let him do / let him make
yap**alım**	let us do / let us make
yap**sınlar**	let them do / let them make

- Koş**ayım**   Let me run
- Gid**eyim**   Let me go
- Yürü**sün**   Let him walk
- Git**sin**   Let her go
- Oku**yalım**   Let us read
- Gel**sinler**   Let them come

- **Gidelim mi?**   Shall we go?
- **Okusun mu?**   Shall he read?
- **Yürüsünler mi?**   Shall they walk?
- **Okuyayım mı?**   Shall I read?

◆ IMPERATIVE

Infinitive	Imperative		
	singular	**plural**	
gelmek (coming, to come)	**gel**	gel**in**	come
gitmek (going, to go)	**git**	gid**in**	go
görmek (seeing, to see)	**gör**	gör**ün**	see
okumak (reading, to read)	**oku**	oku**yun**	read
yazmak (writing, to write)	**yaz**	yaz**ın**	write
bakmak (looking, to look)	**bak**	bak**ın**	look

Formal

gelmek	:	geliniz	come (please)
gitmek	:	gidiniz	go (please)
görmek	:	görünüz	see (please)
okumak	:	okuyunuz	read (please)
yazmak	:	yazınız	write (please)
bakmak	:	bakınız	look (please)

Negative

The negative syllable **'me/ma'** is attached directly to the verb stem. Other suffixes are added to it.

Singular	Plural	Formal	
gelme	gelmeyin	gelmeyiniz	don't come
gitme	gitmeyin	gitmeyiniz	don't go
görme	görmeyin	görmeyiniz	don't see
okuma	okumayın	okumayınız	don't read
yazma	yazmayın	yazmayınız	don't write
bakma	bakmayın	bakmayınız	don't look

■ There is a strong stress on the syllable (verb stem) preceding the negative syllable **'me/ma'**.

....

EXERCISE 13

Look at the following words and listen to your CD. Repeat the words in the gaps provided.

1. gelmek	15.yazın	29.gitmeyiniz
2. gel	16.bakmak	30.görme
3. gelin	17.bak	31.görmeyin
4. gitmek	18.geliniz	32.görmeyiniz
5. git	19.gidiniz	33.okuma
6. gidin	20.görünüz	34.okumayın
7. görmek	21.okuyunuz	35.okumayınız
8. gör	22.yazınız	36.yazma
9. görün	23.bakınız	37.yazmayın
10.okumak	24.gelme	38.yazmayınız
11.oku	25.gelmeyin	39.bakma
12.okuyun	26.gelmeyiniz	40.bakmayın
13.yazmak	27.gitme	41.bakmayınız
14.yaz	28.gitmeyin	

....

◆ DERIVED VERBS

Verbs can be derived from substantives or modifiers by the following means.

1. The suffix **'al / el'**

• **az**	little, few, small, not much
• az**al**mak	to lessen, to become less
• **çok**	many, much, very
• çoğ**al**mak	to increase, become more

2. The suffix **'la / le'**

• **geniş**	wide, extensive
• geniş**le**mek	to widen, to expand

3. The suffix **'lan / len'**

• **umut**	hope
• umut**lan**mak	to become hopeful

4. The suffix **'laş / leş'**

• **beyaz**	white
• beyaz**laş**mak	to get white
• **güzel**	beautiful
• güzel**leş**mek	to become beautiful

LESSON 5

♦ THE VERB 'OLMAK : TO BE'

The forms of the Turkish verb 'to be' appear as suffixes. They are never used alone, as separate words (when the verb 'olmak'is used separately it means 'to become, to happen': **hasta olmak** *to become ill*)

PRESENT TENSE FORMS OF 'OLMAK'

Positive

Ben bir doktor**um**	I am a doctor
Ben bir fabrikatör**üm**	I am a manufacturer
Ben bir dalgıc**ım**	I am a diver
Ben bir öğretmen**im**	I am a teacher
Ben bir işçi**yim***	I am a worker
Sen bir doktor**sun**	You are a doctor
Sen bir fabrikatör**sün**	You are a manufacturer
Sen bir dalgıç**sın**	You are a diver
Sen bir öğretmen**sin**	You are a teacher
Sen bir işçi**sin**	You are a worker
O bir doktor**dur**	He/She is a doctor
O bir fabrikatör**dür**	He/She is a manufacturer
O bir dalgıç**tır**	He/She is a diver
O bir öğretmen**dir**	He/She is a teacher
O bir işçi**dir**	He/She is a worker
Biz doktor**uz**	We are (the) doctors
Biz fabrikatör**üz**	We are (the) manufacturers
Biz dalgıc**ız**	We are (the) divers
Biz öğretmen**iz**	We are (the) teachers
Biz işçi**yiz***	We are (the) workers

Siz doktor**sunuz**	You are (the) doctors
Siz fabrikatör**sünüz**	You are (the) manufacturers
Siz dalgıç**sınız**	You are (the) divers
Siz öğretmen**siniz**	You are (the) teachers
Siz işçi**siniz**	You are (the) workers
Onlar doktor**dur**	They are (the) doctors
Onlar doktor**durlar**	They are (the) doctors
Onlar doktor**lardır**	They are (the) doctors
Onlar fabrikatör**dür**	They are (the) manufacturers
Onlar fabrikatör**dürler**	They are (the) manufacturers
Onlar fabrikatör**lerdir**	They are (the) manufacturers
Onlar dalgıç**tır**	They are (the) divers
Onlar dalgıç**tırlar**	They are (the) divers
Onlar dalgıç**lardır**	They are (the) divers
Onlar öğretmen**dir**	They are (the) teachers
Onlar öğretmen**dirler**	They are (the) teachers
Onlar öğretmen**lerdir**	They are (the) teachers
Onlar işçi**dir**	They are (the) workers
Onlar işçi**dirler**	They are (the) workers
Onlar işçi**lerdir**	They are (the) workers

* The first letter(**y**) in the suffix is a buffer [the buffers (**y**, **n**, or **s**) are used to avoid the contact between two vowels following each other]

Negative Form

Ben bir doktor **değilim**	I am **not** a doctor
Sen bir doktor **değilsin**	You **are not** a doctor
O bir doktor **değildir**	He(she) **is not** a doctor
Biz doktor **değiliz**	We **are not** (the) doctors
Siz doktor **değilsiniz**	You **are not** (the) doctors
Onlar doktor **değiller**	They **are not** (the) doctors
Onlar doktor **değildir(ler)**	They **are not** (the) doctors

Questions

Ben bir doktor **muyum?**	Am I a doctor?
Ben bir fabrikatör **müyüm?**	Am I a manufacturer?
Ben bir dalgıç **mıyım?**	Am I a diver?
Ben bir öğretmen **miyim?**	Am I a teacher?
Ben bir işçi **miyim?**	Am I a worker?
Sen bir doktor **musun?**	Are you a doctor?
Sen bir fabrikatör **müsün?**	Are you a manufacturer?
Sen bir dalgıç **mısın?**	Are you a diver?
Sen bir öğretmen **misin?**	Are you a teacher?
O bir doktor **mu(dur)?**	Is he/she a doctor?
O bir fabrikatör **mü(dür)?**	Is he/she a manufacturer?
O bir dalgıç **mı(dır)?**	Is he/she a diver?
O bir öğretmen **mi(dir)?**	Is he/she a teacher?
Biz doktor **muyuz?**	Are we (the) doctors?
Biz fabrikatör **müyüz?**	Are we (the) manufacturers?
Biz dalgıç **mıyız?**	Are we (the) divers?
Biz öğretmen **miyiz?**	Are we (the) teachers?
Siz doktor **musunuz?**	Are you (the) doctors?
Siz fabrikatör **müsünüz?**	Are you (the) manufacturers?
Siz dalgıç **mısınız?**	Are you (the) divers?
Siz öğretmen **misiniz?**	Are you (the) teachers?
Onlar doktor **mu(dur)?**	Are they (the) doctors?
Onlar doktorlar **mı(dır)?**	Are they (the) doctors?
Onlar doktor **mudurlar?**	Are they (the) doctors?
Onlar fabrikatör **mü(dür)?**	Are they (the) manufacturers?
Onlar fabrikatörler **mi(dir)?**	Are they (the) manufacturers?
Onlar fabrikatör **müdürler?**	Are they (the) manufacturers?
Onlar dalgıç **mı(dır)?**	Are they (the) divers?
Onlar dalgıçlar **mı(dır)?**	Are they (the) divers?
Onlar dalgıç **mıdırlar?**	Are they (the) divers?
Onlar öğretmen **mi(dir)?**	Are they (the) teachers?
Onlar öğretmenler **mi(dir)?**	Are they (the) teachers?
Onlar öğretmen **midirler?**	Are they (the) teachers?

Negative interrogative

Ben bir doktor **değil miyim?**
Sen bir doktor **değil misin?**
O bir doktor **değil mi(dir)?**
Biz doktor **değil miyiz?**

Siz doktor **değil misiniz?**
Onlar doktor **değil midir(ler)?**

Third Person Form

☞ Note that the present tense form of the verb '**to be**' appears as the suffix '**dır / dir / dur / dür**' in the third person singular and plural.

■ When the vowel in the final syllable of the verb is '**a**' or '**ı**', the vowel in the suffix appears as '**ı**'.

- • ... **yaşlıdır**   ... is/are old
- • ... **aslandır**   ... is/are (the) lion(s)

■ When the vowel in the final syllable of the verb is '**e**' or '**i**', the vowel in the suffix appears as '**i**'.

- • ... **güzeldir**   ... is/are pretty, beautiful
- • ... **çirkindir**   ... is/are ugly

■ When the vowel in the final syllable of the verb is '**o**' or '**u**', the vowel in the suffix appears as '**u**'.

- • ... **sarhoştur**   ... is/are drunk
- • ... **uzundur**   ... is/are tall, long

■ When the vowel in the final syllable of the verb is '**ö**' or '**ü**', the vowel in the suffix appears as '**ü**'.

- • ... **sürücüdür**   ... is/are (the) driver(s)
- • ... **önsözdür**   ... is/are (the) preface(s), introduction(s)

♦BUFFERS

Turkish has three buffers used between two vowels: **y, n** and **s**.

A) **banka** (the) bank   **banka<u>y</u>a**   to the bank

B) **cadde** (the) street **Atatürk Cadd<u>e</u>si** Atatürk Street
    fırça (the) brush   **saç fırça<u>s</u>ı**   hair brush (*)

C) **Saç fırçası<u>n</u>a**   to the hair brush
    Atatürk Caddesi<u>n</u>e to the Atatürk Street

___

(*) **Atatürk caddesi, saç fırçası :**

___

■ When the first noun modifies a second one:

➤ When the second noun ends in a consonant, it takes the suffix **'ı/i/u/ü'**.
➤ When the second noun ends in a vowel, it takes the buffer **'s'** between the noun and the suffix.

• Tepebaşı Otel**i**   Tepebaşı Hotel
• İstiklal cadde**si**   İstiklal Street

∙∙∙

🔘 EXERCISE 14

Look at the following sentences and listen to your CD. Repeat the sentences in the gaps provided.

1. Ben bir doktorum
2. Sen bir fabrikatörsün
3. O bir dalgıçtır
4. Biz öğretmeniz
5. Siz işçisiniz
6. Onlar doktordur
7. Onlar fabrikatördürler
8. Onlar dalgıçlardır
9. Ben bir doktor değilim
10. Sen bir doktor değilsin
11. O bir doktor değildir
12. Biz doktor değiliz
13. Siz doktor değilsiniz
14. Onlar doktor değiller
15. Onlar doktor değildir
16. Onlar doktor değildirler
17. Ben bir doktor muyum?
18. Sen bir fabrikatör müsün?
19. O bir dalgıç mı?
20. O bir dalgıç mıdır?
21. Biz öğretmen miyiz?
22. Siz öğretmen misiniz?
23. Onlar doktor mu?
24. Onlar doktor mudur?
25. Onlar doktor mudurlar?
26. Onlar fabrikatörler midir?
27. Onlar fabrikatörler mi?
28. Onlar dalgıç mıdırlar?
29. Onlar öğretmen midir?
30. Onlar öğretmen midirler?

EXERCISE 15
Complete the following with the suitable form of '**to be**'

1. Ben bir şoför.....
2. Ben bir mühendis....
3. Ben bir marangoz.....
4. Ben bir aşçı....
5. Sen bir şoför.....
6. Sen bir mühendis....
7. Sen bir marangoz.....
8. Sen bir aşçı.....
9. O bir aşçı....
10. O bir şoför.....
11. O bir mühendis....
12. O bir marangoz.....
13. O bir aşçı....
14. Biz şoför.....
15. Biz mühendis....
16. Biz marangoz.....
17. Biz aşçı....
18. Siz şoför.....
19. Siz mühendis....

20. Siz marangoz.....
21. Siz aşçı....
22. Onlar şoför.....
23. Onlar mühendis....
24. Onlar marangoz.....
25. Onlar aşçı....
26. Ben bir şoför mü.... ?
27. Sen bir mühendis mi..... ?
28. O bir marangoz mu...... ?
29. Biz aşçı mı..... ?

♦ POSSESSIVE CASE

Possessive Pronouns

Ben	I	Benim	My
Sen	You	Senin	Your
O	He, She, It	Onun	His, Her, Its
Biz	We	Bizim	Our
Siz	You	Sizin	Your
Onlar	They	Onların	Their
Kim?	Who?	Kimin?	Whose?

■ When the possessive pronoun is followed by a noun, the noun takes 'possessive suffix, too.

- defter   notebook
- bilgisayar computer
- okul   school
- ödül   prize
- bahçe   garden
- halı   carpet

- ben**im** defter**im**   my notebook
- ben**im** bilgisayar**ım**   my computer
- ben**im** okul**um**   my school
- ben**im** ödül**üm**   my prize
- ben**im** bahçe**m**   my garden
- ben**im** hal**ım**   my carpet

- sen**in** defter**in**   your notebook
- sen**in** bilgisayar**ın**   your computer
- sen**in** okul**un**   your school
- sen**in** ödül**ün**   your prize
- sen**in** bahçe**n**   your garden
- sen**in** hal**ın**   your carpet

- o**nun** defter**i**   his (her) notebook
- o**nun** bilgisayar**ı**   his (her) computer
- o**nun** okul**u**   his (her) school
- o**nun** ödül**ü**   his (her) prize
- o**nun** bahçe**si**   his (her) garden
- o**nun** hal**ısı**   his (her) carpet

- biz**im** defter**imiz**   our notebook
- biz**im** bilgisayar**ımız**   our computer
- biz**im** okul**umuz**   our school
- biz**im** ödül**ümüz**   our prize
- biz**im** bahçe**miz**   our garden
- biz**im** hal**ımız**   our carpet

- siz**in** defter**iniz**   your notebook
- siz**in** bilgisayar**ınız**   your computer
- siz**in** okul**unuz**   your school
- siz**in** ödül**ünüz**   your prize
- siz**in** bahçe**niz**   your garden
- siz**in** hal**ınız**   your carpet

- onlar**ın** defter**i**   their notebook
- onlar**ın** bilgisayar**ı**   their computer
- onlar**ın** okul**u**   their school
- onlar**ın** ödül**ü**   their prize

- onların bahçe**si**   their garden
- onların halı**sı**   their carpet

■ When the noun is plural, the possessive suffix is attached to the plural suffix.

- benim defterler**im**   my notebooks
- senin bilgisayarlar**ın**   your computers
- onun ödüll**eri**   his(her) prizes
- bizim bahçeler**imiz**   our gardens
- sizin halılar**ınız**   your carpets
- onların kalemler**i**   their pens (or pencils)

Onun köpeği çok iyi futbol oynar
(His dog plays football very well)

■ The possessive pronouns may be omitted.

- **defterim** — my notebook
- **defterin** — your notebook
- **defteri** — his/her notebook (or: their notebook)
- **defterimiz** — our notebook
- **defterleri** — their notebooks (or: his/her notebooks)

Compounds

- Ali'**nin** kitab**ı** — Ali's book; the book of Ali
- Tom'**un** defter**i** — Tom's notebook; the notebook of Tom
- çocuğ**un** eli — the child's hand; the hand of the child
- adam**ın** yüz**ü** — the man's face; the face of the man
- kadın**ın** saç**ı** — the woman's hair; the hair of the woman
- otel**in** oda**sı**(*) — the hotel's room; the room of the hotel
- şirket**in** müdür**ü** — the company's manager; the manager of the company
- fırın**ın** un**u** — the bakery's flour; the flour of the bakery
- terzi**nin** iğne**si** (*) — the tailor's spindle; the spindle of tailor

(*) The above suffixes (**sı / si**) must be distinguished from the suffixes in the noun-noun compounds:

- okul**un** bahçe**si** — the garden **of** the school
- okul bahçe**si** — the school garden

- otel**in** oda**sı** — the room **of** the hotel
- otel oda**sı** — the hotel room

- **duvar halısı** — the wall carpet
- (**benim**) duvar halı**m** — my wall carpet

- **diş fırçası** — the toothbrush
- (**senin**) diş fırça**n** — your toothbrush

ev	house	evin	the house's, of the house
bilgisayar	computer	bilgisayarın	the computer's, of the computer
gazete	newspaper	gazetenin	the newspaper's, of the newspaper
araba	car	arabanın	the car's, of the car
okul	school	okulun	the school's, of the school
göz	eye	gözün	the eye's, of the eye
radyo	radio	radyonun	the radio's, of the radio
ütü	iron	ütünün	the iron's, of the iron

Kendi

The word **'kendi'** means 'self'. It is often used with possessive constructions.

- (benim) **kendi** bilgisayarım   my own computer
- (senin) **kendi** bilgisayarın   your own computer

☞ Note that 'possessive pronouns (benim, senin, etc.)' may be omitted.

Aslı'nın kendi bilgisayarı var

Kendim, Kendin, ...

kendim	myself
kendin	yourself
kendi(si)	himself / herself
kendimiz	ourselves
kendiniz	yourselves
kendileri	themselves

- **Onu kendim onardım.**
  I repaired it myself

Tek başıma, Tek başına... (or: Kendi başıma ,.....)

tek başıma	by myself
(sen) tek başına	by yourself
(o) tek başına	by himself / herself
tek başımıza	by ourselves
tek başınıza	by yourselves
tek başlarına	by themselves

THE SUFFIX '-Kİ'

1. As an adjective, it is attached to a substantive.

- önce**ki** gün   previous day
- dün akşam**ki** kar   yesterday evening's snow

2. As an adjectival expression, it is attached to a locative suffix.

- masa**daki** kitap   the book on the table
- bahçe**deki** çiçekler the flowers in the garden
- elim**deki** kalem   the pen in my hand

-Şu kitabı verir misiniz lütfen.
-Give me that book, please.

-Hangi kitap?
-Which book?

• -Masanın üzerindeki kitap.
-The book on the table.

3. As the equivalents to English 'Possessive Pronouns (mine, yours …)', it is attached to the possessive forms of nouns and personal pronouns.

• Bu kalem **benimki**(dir)   This pen is mine.
• **Seninki** nerede(dir)?   Where is yours?
• **Onunki** burada(dır).   His/hers/its is here.

• Bunlar **bizimkiler**(dir).   These are ours.
• Bu **bizimki**(dir).   This is ours.
• Şunlar **sizinkiler**(dir).   Those are yours.
• Şu **sizinki**(dir).   That is yours.
• **Onlarınki(ler)** masanın üzerinde(dir).   Theirs are on the table.
• Bu **onlarınki**(dir).   This is theirs.

POSSESSIVE PRONOUNS

Singular		plural
benim**ki**	mine	benimki**ler**
senin**ki**	yours	seninki**ler**
onun**ki**	his / hers	onunki**ler**
bizim**ki**	ours	bizimki**ler**
sizin**ki**	yours	sizinki**ler**
onların**ki**	theirs	onlarınki**ler**

• **Bu, benim kitabım(dır).**   This is my book.
• **Bu kitap, benimki(dir).**   This book is mine.
• **Bunlar, benim kitaplarım(dır).**   These are my books.
• **Bu kitaplar, benimkiler(dir).**   These books are mine.

- Bu benimki, bu da seninki.

☞ Note that '-ki' does not conform to vowel harmony.

■ **'ki'** is also used as relative in an unfinished expression:

- **O kadar çok gezdim ki...**   I travelled so much that....
- **Öyle(sine) güzeldi ki...**   She was so beautiful that...

EXERCISE 16

Look at the following list and listen to your CD. Repeat in the gaps provided

1. benim defterim
2. senin bilgisayarın
3. onun telefonu
4. bizim ödülümüz
5. sizin bahçeniz
6. onların halısı
7. benim defterlerim
8. senin halıların
9. çocuğun eli
10. kadının saçı
11. otelin odası
12. okul bahçesi
13. otel odası
14. kendi bilgisayarım
15. kendi arabası
16. dün akşamki kar
17. masadaki kitap
18. bu kalem benimki
19. şu kitap seninki
20. öylesine güzel ki ...

EXERCISE 17

A) Add the necessary possessive suffixes to the following words and try to translate.

Example: Ben - araba :   Ben**im** araba**m** (my car)

1. Ben - kalem   :..
2. Ben - kitap   :..
3. Ben - öğrenciler :..
4. Sen - masa   :..
5. Sen - gözlük   :..
6. O   - televizyon :..
7. O   - bardak   :..
8. Biz - dergi   :..
9. Biz - kitap   :..
10. Biz - sözlük   :..
11. Siz - çatal   :..
12. Siz - kaşık   :..

13. Siz - kitaplar :...

14. Siz - sözlükler :...

15. Onlar- kedi :...

16. Onlar- köpek :...

B) Write the following in Turkish.

1. The man's hair
2. The woman's hand
3. Okan's dictionary
4. Orçun's book
5. My own car
6. Your own magazine
7. This car is mine
8. That car is yours
9. I repaired it by myself

···

♦ VAR , YOK
[there is(n't) / are(n't) , (not) to have (got)]

The words 'var' and 'yok' are always followed by the verb 'to be' which may be omitted in the present tense.

var	:	extant, in existence
yok	:	non-extant, not in existence

■ These words have two principal uses:

1. Their first function is to express possession.

- **(Benim) bir arabam var(dır).**
  I have (got) a car.

- **Atakan'ın bir evi var(dır).**
  Atakan has (got) a house.

- **Kız kardeşiniz var mı(dır)?**
  Have you got a sister / Do you have a sister ?

- **Pınar'ın üç çocuğu var(dır).**
  Pınar has (got) three children.

- **Ege'nin erkek kardeşleri var mı(dır)?**
  Has Ege got any brothers / Does she have any brothers ?

- **Aslı'nın hiç erkek kardeşi yok(tur).**
  Aslı hasn't (got) any brothers.

- **Onun bir kız arkadaşı vardı.**
  He had a girl-friend.

- **Hiç paran(ız) var mı(dır)?**
  Have you got any money / Do you have any money ?

- **Merve'nin çok parası var(dır).**
  Merve has (got) a lot of money.

- **(Senin) Babanın arabası var mı(dır)?**
  Has your father got a car / Does your father have a car ?

- **Gonca'nın hiç çocuğu yok(tur).**
  Gonca has (got) no children.

- **Orhan'ın hiç parası yok(tur).**
  Orhan hasn't (got) any money.

- **Sizde (Yanınızda) hiç para yok mu(dur)?**
  Haven't you got any money with you ? /
  Don't you have any money with you ?

- **Kimin beş çocuğu var(dır)?**
  Who has (got) five children?

2. Their second function is to express the English 'there is / are (not)'

- **Masanın üstünde bir kitap var(dır).**
  There is a book on the table.

- **Masanın üstünde hiç kitap var mı(dır)?**
  Are there any books on the table?

- **Başka seçenek(ler) var mı(dır)?**
  Are there any other alternatives?

- **Masanın üstünde beş kitap var(dır).**
  There are five books on the table.

- **Evde bir televizyon ve bir yatak var(dır).**
  There are a television and a bed in the house.

- **Orada hiç okul yok(tur).**
  There aren't any schools there.

- **Orada okul var mı(dır)?**
  Is there any school there?

- **Okulda hiç öğrenci yok(tur).**
  There aren't any students in the school.

- **Burada (hiç) kimse yok(tur).**
  There isn't anybody here.

- **Bardakta hiç çay var mı(dır) ?**
  Is there any tea in the glass ?

- **Bardakta hiç çay yok(tur)**
  There isn't any tea in the glass.

- **Bardakta hiç su yok mu(dur)?**
  Isn't there any water in the glass?

Özge'nin minik bir kedisi var

....

💿 EXERCISE 18

Write the following sentences in Turkish and listen to your CD for the correct answers. Repeat the sentences in the gaps provided.

1. We've got a new car / We have a new car.
2. Okan's got a headache / Okan has a headache.
3. Have you got any money? / Do you have any money?
4. Have you got a light ? / Do you have a light ?
5. I haven't got my key. / I don't have my key.
6. There is a house there.
7. There is a table in the room.
8. There isn't anybody in the house.
9. There are two lambs in the garden.
10. There aren't any teachers in the school.

LESSON 6

♦ SIMPLE PAST TENSE

The Turkish 'Simple Past Tense' is used to talk about an action that is finished or has been completed in the past. It can also be used as an equivalent to the English 'Present Perfect Tense'.

(*)
(ben) geldim   I came , I did come , I have come

(*) Personal pronouns may be omitted.

■ All the simple past tense suffixes (which are the past tense forms of 'to be') begin with the variable consonant **'t/d'**.

  1. The suffix begins with '**d**' when the verb stem ends in a voiced consonant.
  2. The suffix begins with '**t**' when the verb stem ends in a voiceless consonant.
  3. The suffix begins with '**d**' when the verb stem ends in a vowel.

■ When the dominant vowel in the verb stem is '**e**' or '**i**':

gelmek	coming, to come
seçmek	to choose, to select, to elect
elemek	eliminate, sift, select
silmek	to wipe, to erase
gitmek	to go

1	2	3
geldim	seçtim	eledim
geldin	seçtin	eledin
geldi	seçti	eledi
geldik	seçtik	eledik
geldiniz	seçtiniz	elediniz
geldiler	seçtiler	elediler
sildim	gittim	
sildin	gittin	
sildi	gitti	
sildik	gittik	
sildiniz	gittiniz	
sildiler	gittiler	

■ When the dominant vowel is 'a' or 'ı':

dalmak	to dive
bakmak	to look
kırmak	to break
alışmak	to get used to

daldım	baktım
daldın	baktın
daldı	baktı
daldık	baktık
daldınız	baktınız
daldılar	baktılar

kırdım	alıştım
kırdın	alıştın
kırdı	alıştı
kırdık	alıştık
kırdınız	alıştınız
kırdılar	alıştılar

Bora yarışı kazandı

■ When the dominant vowel is 'o' or 'u'

olmak	to be
koşmak	to run
kurtulmak	to escape, to get free, to be saved
konuşmak	to talk, to speak

ol**dum**	koş**tum**
ol**dun**	koş**tun**
ol**du**	koş**tu**
ol**duk**	koş**tuk**
ol**dunuz**	koş**tunuz**
ol**dular**	koş**tular**

kurtul**dum**	konuş**tum**
kurtul**dun**	konuş**tun**
kurtul**du**	konuş**tu**
kurtul**duk**	konuş**tuk**
kurtul**dunuz**	konuş**tunuz**
kurtul**dular**	konuş**tular**

■ When the dominant vowel is 'ö' or 'ü'

bölmek	to separate, to divide
öpmek	to kiss
götürmek	to take away, to lead
gözükmek	to be seen

böl**düm**	öp**tüm**
böl**dün**	öp**tün**
böl**dü**	öp**tü**
böl**dük**	öp**tük**
böl**dünüz**	öp**tünüz**
böl**düler**	öp**tüler**

götür**düm**	gözük**tüm**
götür**dün**	gözük**tün**
götür**dü**	gözük**tü**

götür**dük**	gözük**tük**
götür**dünüz**	gözük**tünüz**
götür**düler**	gözük**tüler**

- Çocuğunuzu unuttunuz !

Negative

The simple past tense suffix is preceded by the negative syllable '**me / ma**'.

• gel**me**dim	I didn't come, I haven't come
• seç**me**din	you didn't choose, you haven't chosen
• sil**me**di	he didn't wipe, I haven't wiped
• git**me**dik	we didn't go, we haven't gone
• ele**me**diniz	you didn't select, you haven't selected
• dal**ma**dılar	they didn't dive, they haven't dived
• bak**ma**dım	I didn't look, I haven't looked
• kır**ma**dın	you didn't break, you haven't broken
• alış**ma**dı	she didn't get used to, she haven't get used to
• götür**me**dik	we didn't lead, we haven't led
• gözük**me**diniz	you didn't seem, you haven't seemed
• böl**me**diler	they didn't divide, they haven't divided
• öp**me**diler	they didn't kiss, they haven't kissed

Interrogative

- geldim **mi**?   did I come?, have I come?
- aldık **mı**?   did we take?, have we taken?
- gördün **mü**?   did you see?, have you seen?
- okudunuz **mu**?   did you read?, have you read?
- **Kim** geldi?   who came?, who has come?
- **Ne zaman** geldiniz? when did you come?, when have you come?
- **Nasıl** geldiler?   how did they come?, how have they come?
- **Niye** gelmediniz?   why didn't you come?, why haven't you come?
- **Neden** gelmediniz?   why didn't you come?, why haven't you come?

Negative Interrogative:
The interrogative sign is '**mı / mi**'

- Gelmedim **mi**?   Didn't I come?,   Haven't I come?
- Almadık **mı**?   Didn't we take?, Haven't we taken?
- Görmedin **mi**?   Didn't you see?, Haven't you seen?
- Okumadınız **mı**?   Didn't you read?, Haven't you read?

- Geldin **mi**?   Did you come?, Have you come?
- Sen **mi** geldin   Is it you who came?
- Dün geldin **mi**?   Did you come yesterday?
- Dün **mü** geldin?   Did you come <u>yesterday</u>?

....

EXERCISE 19

A. Complete the following with the suitable past tense suffix and translate.

1. Ben dün erken uyan.....
2. Sen yalnız mı git..... ?
3. Ulaş dün işe geç kal....
4. Okan ve Ben dün çok para harca....
5. Atakan ve sen filmi beğenme.....
6. Okan ve Atakan partiden erken ayrıl.....

B. Translate the following sentences:

1. Aslı bought a dress yesterday.
2. What did you do yesterday evening ?
3. We didn't invite her to the party.
4. Why didn't you phone me on Monday ?
5. They left the party at 10 o'clock.

 ## EXERCISE 20

Look at the expressions in the following list and listen to your CD. Repeat the expressions in the gaps provided.

1. Geldim
2. Gelmedim
3. Geldim mi?
4. Gelmedim mi
5. Ben mi geldim?
6. Seçtin
7. Seçmedin
8. Seçtin mi
9. Seçmedin mi?
10. Sen mi seçtin?
11. Kırdı
12. Kırmadı
13. Kırdı mı?
14. Kırmadı mı?
15. O mu kırdı?
16. Alıştık
17. Alışmadık
18. Alıştık mı?
19. Alışmadık mı?
20. Biz mi alıştık?
21. Kurtuldunuz
22. Kurtulmadınız
23. Kurtuldunuz mu?
24. Kurtulmadınız mı?
25. Siz mi kurtuldunuz?
26. Konuştular
27. Konuşmadılar
28. Konuştular mı?
29. Konuşmadılar mı?
30. Onlar mı konuştular?
31. Götürdün
32. Götürmedin
33. Götürdün mü?
34. Götürmedin mi?
35. Sen mi götürdün?
36. Gözüktü
37. Gözükmedi
38. Gözüktü mü?
39. Gözükmedi mi?
40. O mu gözüktü?

♦ Past Tense Forms of 'OLMAK : TO BE'

Ben öğretmen	**idim**	I **was** (the) teacher
Sen öğretmen	**idin**	You **were** (the) teacher
O öğretmen	**idi**	He(She) **was** (the) teacher
Biz öğretmen	**idik**	We **were** (the) teachers
Siz öğretmen	**idiniz**	You **were** (the) teachers
Onlar öğretmen	**idiler**	They **were** (the) teachers

■ The past tense forms of 'to be'(**idim, idin, idi, idik, idiniz, idiler**) are usually used as suffixes.
Study the following examples :

Positive:

Ben bir doktor**dum**	I was a doctor
Ben bir fabrikatör**düm**	I was a manufacturer
Ben bir dalgıç**tım**	I was a diver
Ben bir öğretmen**dim**	I was a teacher
Ben bir işçi**ydim**(*)	I was a worker

Sen bir doktor**dun**	You were a doctor
Sen bir fabrikatör**dün**	You were manufacturer
Sen bir dalgıç**tın**	You were a diver
Sen bir öğretmen**din**	You were a teacher
Sen bir işçi**ydin** (*)	You were a worker

O bir doktor**du**	He (She) was a doctor
O bir fabrikatör**dü**	He (She) was a manufacturer
O bir dalgıç**tı**	He (he) was a diver
O bir öğretmen**di**	He (She) was a teacher
O bir işçi**ydi** (*)	He (She) was a worker

Biz doktor**duk**	We were (the) doctors
Biz fabrikatör**dük**	We were (the) manufacturers
Biz dalgı**cız**	We were (the) divers

Biz öğretmen**dik**	We were (the) teachers
Biz işçi**ydik** (*)	We were (the) workers
Siz doktor**dunuz**	You were (the) doctors
Siz fabrikatör**dünüz**	You were (the) manufacturers
Siz dalgıç**tınız**	You were (the) divers
Siz öğretmen**diniz**	You were (the) teachers
Siz işçi**ydiniz** (*)	You were (the) workers
Onlar doktor**du**	They were (the) doctors
Onlar doktor**dular**	They were (the) doctors
Onlar doktor**lardı**	They were (the) doctors
Onlar fabrikatör**dü**	They were (the) manufacturers
Onlar fabrikatör**düler**	They were (the) manufacturers
Onlar fabrikatör**lerdi**	They were (the) manufacturers
Onlar dalgıç**tı**	They were (the) divers
Onlar dalgıç**tılar**	They were (the) divers
Onlar dalgıç**lardı**	They were (the) divers
Onlar öğretmen**di**	They were (the) teachers
Onlar öğretmen**diler**	They were (the) teachers
Onlar öğretmen**lerdi**	They were (the) teachers
Onlar işçi**ydi** (*)	They were (the) workers
Onlar işçi**ydiler** (*)	They were (the) workers
Onlar işçi**lerdi**	They were (the) workers
Benim bir arabam <u>vardı</u>	I had a car
Odada iki yatak <u>vardı</u>	There were two bed in the room

(*) When the main word ends in a vowel, the buffer '**y**' is inserted between that vowel and the past suffix.

Negative

Ben bir doktor **<u>değildim</u>**	I **was** <u>**not**</u> a doctor
Sen bir doktor **<u>değildin</u>**	You **were** <u>**not**</u> a doctor
O bir doktor **<u>değildi</u>**	Ye(She) **was** <u>**not**</u> a doctor
Biz doktor **<u>değildik</u>**	We **were** <u>**not**</u> (the) doctors
Siz doktor **<u>değildiniz</u>**	You **were** <u>**not**</u> (the) doctors
Onlar doktor **<u>değillerdi</u>**	They **were** <u>**not**</u> (the) doctors
Onlar doktor **<u>değildi</u>(ler)**	They **were** <u>**not**</u> (the) doctors

Hiç param yok**tu**   I didn't have any money
Tabakta hiç peynir yok**tu** There wasn't any cheese on the plate

Interrogative

Ben bir doktor **muydum?**	Was I a doctor?
Ben bir fabrikatör **müydüm?**	Was I a manufacturer?
Ben bir dalgıç **mıydım?**	Was I a diver?
Ben bir öğretmen **miydim?**	Was I a teacher?
Ben bir işçi **miydim?**	Was I a worker?
Sen bir doktor **muydun?**	Were you a doctor?
Sen bir fabrikatör **müydün?**	Were you a manufacturer?
Sen bir dalgıç **mıydın?**	Were you a diver?
Sen bir öğretmen **miydin?**	Were you a teacher?
O bir doktor **muydu?**	Was he(she) a doctor?
O bir fabrikatör **müydü?**	Was he(she) a manufacturer?
O bir dalgıç **mıydı?**	Was he(she) a diver?
O bir öğretmen **miydi?**	Was he(she) a teacher?
Biz doktor **muyduk?**	Were we (the) doctors?
Biz fabrikatör **müydük?**	Were we (the) manufacturers?
Biz dalgıç **mıydık?**	Were we (the) divers?
Biz öğretmen **miydik?**	Were we (the) teachers?
Siz doktor **muydunuz?**	Were you (the) doctors?
Siz fabrikatör **müydünüz?**	Were you (the) manufacturers?
Siz dalgıç **mıydınız?**	Were you (the) divers?
Siz öğretmen **miydiniz?**	Were you (the) teachers?
Onlar doktor **muydu?**	Were they (the) doctors?
Onlar doktorlar **mıydı?**	Were they (the) doctors?
Onlar doktor **muydular?**	Were they (the) doctors?
Onlar fabrikatör **müydü?**	Were they (the) manufacturers?
Onlar fabrikatörler **miydi?**	Were they (the) manufacturers?
Onlar fabrikatör **müydüler?**	Were they (the) manufacturers?
Onlar dalgıç **mıydı?**	Were they (the) divers?

Onlar dalgıçlar **mıydı?**	Were they (the) divers?
Onlar dalgıç **mıydılar?**	Were they (the) divers?
Onlar öğretmen **miydi?**	Were they (the) teachers?
Onlar öğretmenler **miydi?**	Were they (the) teachers?
Onlar öğretmen **miydiler?**	Were they (the) teachers?

Negative Interrogative

Ben bir doktor **değil miydim?**
Sen bir doktor **değil miydin?**
O bir doktor **değil miydi?**
Biz doktor **değil miydik?**
Siz doktor **değil miydiniz?**
Onlar doktor **değil miydiler?**

••

EXERCISE 21

Complete the following with the suitable past tense suffix and translate.

1. Selin dün işte.....
2. Neden sen o kadar kızgın....
3. Ben mühendis....
4. Biz aç değil....
5. Siz çok aç.....
6. Onlar bana çok kızgın......

••

EXERCISE 22

Look at the sentences in the following list and listen to your CD. Repeat the sentences in the gaps provided.

1. Ben bir doktordum.
2. Sen bir fabrikatördün.
3. O bir dalgıçtı.
4. Biz öğretmendik.
5. Siz işçiydiniz.
6. Onlar doktordular.
7. Ben bir doktor muydum?
8. Sen bir fabrikatör müydün?
9. O bir dalgıç mıydı?
10. Biz öğretmen miydik?
11. Siz fabrikatör müydünüz?
12. Onlar doktor muydular?
13. Ben bir doktor değil miydim?
14. Sen bir doktor değil miydin?
15. O bir doktor değil miydi?
16. Biz doktor değil miydik?
17. Siz doktor değil miydiniz?
18. Onlar doktor değil miydiler?
19. Sen bir doktor değildin.
20. O bir doktor değildi.

◆ PRESENT CONTINUOUS TENSE

(Ben)	verb stem + (ı / i / u / ü) + yor + um
(Sen)	verb stem + (ı / i / u / ü) + yor + sun
(O)	verb stem + (ı / i / u / ü) + yor
(Biz)	verb stem + (ı / i / u / ü) + yor + uz
(Siz)	verb stem + (ı / i / u / ü) + yor + sunuz
(Onlar)	verb stem + (ı / i / u / ü) + yor + lar

- **bak**mak   to look

(Ben)	bak**ıyorum**	I am looking
(Sen)	bak**ıyorsun**	you are looking
(O)	bak**ıyor**	he (she, it) is looking
(Biz)	bak**ıyoruz**	we are looking
(Siz)	bak**ıyorsunuz**	you are looking
(Onlar)	bak**ıyorlar**	they are looking

- **gel**mek   to come

(Ben)	gel**iyorum**	I am coming
(Sen)	gel**iyorsun**	you are coming
(O)	gel**iyor**	he (she, it) is coming
(Biz)	gel**iyoruz**	we are coming
(Siz)	gel**iyorsunuz**	you are coming
(Onlar)	gel**iyorlar**	they are coming

- **oku**mak   to read

(Ben)	oku**yorum**	I am reading
(Sen)	oku**yorsun**	you are reading
(O)	oku**yor**	he (she, it) is reading
(Biz)	oku**yoruz**	we are reading
(Siz)	oku**yorsunuz**	you are reading
(Onlar)	oku**yorlar**	they are reading

- **yürü**mek   to walk

(Ben)	yürü**yorum**	I am walking
(Sen)	yürü**yorsun**	you are walking
(O)	yürü**yor**	he (she, it) is walking
(Biz)	yürü**yoruz**	we are walking
(Siz)	yürü**yorsunuz**	you are walking
(Onlar)	yürü**yorlar**	they are walking

Okan telefonla konuşuyor

İpek koşuyor

Onlar kürek çekiyor(lar)

Bora bisiklete biniyor

Tolga şaşırıyor

Aslı yemek yapıyor

Negative *

In the present continuous tense the negative sign is **m(ı / i / u / ü)**.

(Ben)	**verb stem + m(ı / i / u / ü) + yor um**
(Sen)	**verb stem + m(ı / i / u / ü) + yor sun**
(O)	**verb stem + m(ı / i / u / ü) + yor**
(Biz)	**verb stem + m(ı / i / u / ü) + yor uz**
(Siz)	**verb stem + m(ı / i / u / ü) + yor sunuz**
(Onlar)	**verb stem + m(ı / i / u / ü) + yor lar**

- **(Ben)** **gelmiyorum** — I am not coming
- **(Sen)** **gelmiyorsun** — you are not coming
- **(O)** **gelmiyor** — he (she, it) is not coming
- **(Biz)** **gelmiyoruz** — we are not coming
- **(Siz)** **gelmiyorsunuz** — you are not coming
- **(Onlar)** **gelmiyorlar** — they are not coming

Interrogative

(Ben)	**verb stem + (ı / i / u / ü) + yor mu yum?**
(Sen)	**verb stem + (ı / i / u / ü) + yor mu sun?**
(O)	**verb stem + (ı / i / u / ü) + yor mu?**
(Biz)	**verb stem + (ı / i / u / ü) + yor mu yuz?**
(Siz)	**verb stem + (ı / i / u / ü) + yor mu sunuz?**
(Onlar)	**verb stem + (ı / i / u / ü) + yor lar mı?**

- **(Ben)** **geliyor muyum?** — am I coming?
- **(Sen)** **geliyor musun?** — are you coming?
- **(O)** **geliyor mu?** — is he (she, it) coming?
- **(Biz)** **geliyor muyuz?** — are we coming?
- **(Siz)** **geliyor musunuz?** — are you coming?
- **(Onlar)** **geliyorlar mı?** — are they coming?

Negative interrogative

(Ben)	verb stem + m(ı / i / u / ü) + yor mu yum?
(Sen)	verb stem + m(ı / i / u / ü) + yor mu sun?
(O)	verb stem + m(ı / i / u / ü) + yor mu?
(Biz)	verb stem + m(ı / i / u / ü) + yor mu yuz?
(Siz)	verb stem + m(ı / i / u / ü) + yor mu sunuz?
(Onlar)	verb stem + m(ı / i / u / ü) + yor lar mı?

- (Ben) **gelmiyor muyum?** am I not coming?
- (Sen) **gelmiyor musun?** aren't you coming?
- (O) **gelmiyor mu?** isn't he (she, it) coming?
- (Biz) **gelmiyor muyuz?** aren't we coming?
- (Siz) **gelmiyor musunuz?** aren't you coming?
- (Onlar) **gelmiyorlar mı?** aren't they coming?

The verbs 'gitmek, etmek' in the present continuous tense

The last letter 't' in the stems of these verbs is a variable consonant (**t/d**).

- **gidiyorum** I am going
- **gidiyorsun** you are going
- **gidiyor** he is going
- **gidiyoruz** we are going
- **gidiyorsunuz** you are going
- **gidiyorlar** they are going

- **ediyorum** I am doing
- **ediyorsun** you are doing
- **ediyor** he is doing
- **ediyoruz** we are doing
- **ediyorsunuz** you are doing
- **ediyorlar** they are doing

··

*Negative Verb

Most of the negative signs (or: syllables) begin with '**m**' in Turkish. The second letter of the syllable is ' **e, a, i, ı, ü** or **u**' (due to the vowel harmony rule). The negative syllable is attached directly to the verb stem and other suffixes are added to it.

- gel**me**mek   **not** to come
- gel**mi**yorum   I am not coming
- gel**me**dim   I didn't come(I haven't come)
- oku**mu**yorum   I am not reading
- oku**ma**dım   I didn't read(I haven't read)
- bak**mı**yorum   I am not looking
- götür**mü**yorum   I am not taking away
- otur**mu**yorum   I am not sitting

··

A Special Form of Present Continuous Tense

Infinitive + Locative suffix + Present tense form of 'to be'

gelmekte olmak   :   to be in the act of coming

- (Ben)   **gelmekteyim**   I am coming
- (Sen)   **gelmektesin**   you are coming
- (O)   **gelmektedir**   he is coming
- (Biz)   **gelmekteyiz**   we are coming
- (Siz)   **gelmektesiniz**   you are coming
- (Onlar) **gelmektedirler**   they are coming

Negative

- (Ben)   **gelmekte değilim**   I am not coming
- (Sen)   **gelmekte değilsin**   you are not coming
- (O)   **gelmekte değil(dir)**   he is not coming
- (Biz)   **gelmekte değiliz**   we are not coming
- (Siz)   **gelmekte değilsiniz**   you are not coming
- (Onlar) **gelmekte değiller**   they are not coming

Interrogative

- (Ben)   **gelmekte miyim?**   am I coming?
- (Sen)   **gelmekte misin?**   are you coming?
- (O)   **gelmekte mi(dir)?**   is he coming?
- (Biz)   **gelmekte miyiz?**   are we coming?
- (Siz)   **gelmekte misiniz?**   are you coming?
- (Onlar) **gelmekte midirler?**   are they coming?

EXERCISE 23

Put the verbs in brackets into 'present continuous tense' and listen to your CD for correct answers.

1. Ben kitabı Okan'a .... (vermek)
2. Sen çok iyi araba .... (kullanmak)
3. Şafak Almanca .... (öğrenmek)
4. Umut ve ben sigara .... (i**çme**mek)
5. Siz çok hızlı .... (koşmak)
6. Ulaş ve Buğra televizyondaki filme .... (gülmek)
7. Okan .... (gül**me**mek)
8. Sen kitabı kime .... (vermek)?
9. Onlar nereye .... (gitmek) ?
10. Sen partiye .... (gelmek) ?
11. Siz filmi .... (izlemek) ?

♦ PAST CONTINUOUS TENSE

(Ben) geliyor + dum	I was coming, I used to come
Third person singular, present continuous + **Past tense form of 'to be' (-dum,-dun,.... etc.)**	

- geliyordum   I was coming
- geliyordun   you were coming
- geliyordu   he(she, it) was coming
- geliyorduk   we were coming
- geliyordunuz   you were coming
- geliyorlardı   they were coming

Negative:

- gelmiyordum   I wasn't coming
- gelmiyordun   you weren't coming
- gelmiyordu   he(she, it) wasn't coming
- gelmiyorduk   we weren't coming
- gelmiyordunuz   you weren't coming
- gelmiyorlardı   they weren't coming

Interrogative:

- geliyor muydum?   was I coming?
- geliyor muydun?   were you coming?
- geliyor muydu?   was he(she, it) coming?
- geliyor muyduk?   were we coming?
- geliyor muydunuz?   were you coming?
- geliyorlar mıydı?   were they coming?

Negative Interrogative:

- **gelmiyor muydum?**   wasn't I coming?
- **gelmiyor muydun?**   weren't you coming?
- **gelmiyor muydu?**   wasn't he(she/it) coming?
- **gelmiyor muyduk?**   weren't we coming?
- **gelmiyor muydunuz?**   weren't you coming?
- **gelmiyorlar mıydı?**   weren't they coming?

Onlar güneşleniyorlar

Onlar güneşleniyorlardı

EXERCISE 24

Put the verbs in brackets into 'past continuous tense' and listen to your CD for correct answers.

1.   Ben çok iyi araba .... (kullanmak)
2.   Sen kitabı Ulaş'a .... (vermek)
3.   Tom sigara .... (içmemek)
4.   Umut ve ben Türkçe .... (öğrenmek)
5.   Siz televizyondaki filme .... (gülmek)
6.   Okan .... (gülmemek)
7.   Ulaş ve Buğra çok hızlı .... (koşmak)
8.   Ben hangi kitabı .... (okumak)?
9.   Siz nereye .... (gitmek) ?
10. Onlar iyi Türkçe .... (konuşmak)?
11. Aslı filmi .... (izlemek) ?

LESSON 7

♦ ACCUSATIVE CASE

■ Accusative case is formed by the suffix 'ı / i / u / ü'
■ The substantive to which the accusative suffix is attached is the direct object of a verb.
■ When the substantive ends in a vowel, the buffer 'y' is needed between the vowel and the suffix.

• **kalem**	(the) pen, (the) pencil
• Kalemi gördüm	I saw the pencil
• **masa**	(the) table
• Masayı taşıdılar	They carried the table
• **televizyon**	(the) television
• Televizyonu satın aldım	I bought the television
• **üzüm**	grape
• Üzümü yediniz mi?	Have you eaten the grapes?

■ The plural suffix precedes the accusative suffix.

• **kalemler**	(the) pens
• Kalemleri getirdiniz mi?	Have you brought the pens?
• **masalar**	(the) tables
• Masaları temizlediniz mi?	Did you clean the tables?

When the substantive ends in a variable consonant (**ç, k, p** or **t**);

- ağa**ç**   ağac**ı**   (the) tree
- balı**k**   balı**ğı**   (the) fish
- kita**p**   kita**bı**   (the) book

• Accusative Case of Interrogative Pronouns

Kim?	Who?	**Kimi?**	Whom?
Ne?	What?	**Neyi?**	What?

• Accusative Case of Demonstratives

	objective definite	
bu	**bunu (*)**	this
şu	şu**nu**	that
o	o**nu**	that
bunlar	bunlar**ı**	these
şunlar	şunlar**ı**	those
onlar	onlar**ı**	those

(*)Note that the buffer **'n'** is used with the demonstratives 'bu, şu, o'.

• Accusative Case of Personal Pronouns

ben	I	beni	me
sen	you	seni	you
o	he, she, it	onu	him, her, it
biz	we	bizi	us
siz	you	sizi	you
onlar	they	onları	them

♦ DATIVE , LOCATIVE and ABLATIVE CASES

Dative Case of Nouns

The dative suffix is : **'(y)e / (y)a'**

ev	house	ev**e**	to the house
okul	school	okul**a**	to the school
kedi	cat	kedi**ye**	to the cat
oda	room	oda**ya**	to the room
Ali		Ali'**ye**	to Ali

Aslı, kağıtları hava**ya** atıyor

Dative Case of Personal Pronouns

ben	I	ba**na**	to me
sen	you	sa**na**	to you
o	he, she, it	o**na**	to him, her, it
biz	we	biz**e**	to us
siz	you	siz**e**	to you
onlar	they	onlar**a**	to them

Ablative Case of Nouns

The ablative suffix is : **'den / dan'**

ev	house	ev**den**	from (the) house
araba	car	araba**dan**	from (the) car
otobüs	bus	otobüs**ten**	from (the) bus
ağaç	tree	ağaç**tan**	from (the) tree

Avcı ayı**dan** kaçıyor

Ablative Case of Personal Pronouns

ben	I	ben**den**	from me
sen	you	sen**den**	from you
o	he, she, it	o**ndan**	from him (her/ it)
biz	we	biz**den**	from us
siz	you	siz**den**	from you
onlar	they	onlar**dan**	from them

Locative Case of Nouns (in, on, at)

The locative suffix is : **'d(t)e/d(t)a'**

ev	house, home	ev**de**	in the house, at home
araba	car	araba**da**	in the car
otobüs	bus	otobüs**te**	on the bus
ağaç	tree	ağaç**ta**	in the tree

Onlar otobüs durağı**nda**(lar)

Locative Case of Personal Pronouns

ben	I	ben**de**	at me
sen	you	sen**de**	at you
o	he, she, it	o**nda**	at him, at her, at it
biz	we	biz**de**	at us
siz	you	siz**de**	at you
onlar	they	onlar**da**	at them

DE / DA (too, also)

Orhan **da** geldi.	Orhan came **too**.
Şu kitabı **da** istiyorum.	I **also** want that book.

■ You have to distinguish this word from the locative suffix.
■ This word is used as an independent word but it conforms in vowel harmony to the preceding word.

- Ece **de** gitti. Ece went **too**.
- Aslı'yı **da** gördüm. I have **also** seen Aslı.

■ When it is repeated, it means 'both......and'

- Aslı **da** Okan **da** both Aslı and Okan
- sen **de** ben **de** both you and me

Okan bir iş adamıdır   Ozan **da** bir iş adamıdır

◆ TELLING THE TIME

Saat kaç?	What time is it?

• Saat *	It's ......
• iki	two o'clock.
• onu beş **geçiyor**	five **past** ten
• altıya on **var**	ten **to** six
• yedi **buçuk**	**half past** seven
• üçe **çeyrek var**	**a quarter to** three
• dokuzu **çeyrek geçiyor**	**a quarter past** nine
• (Saat) bir**de**	**at** one (o'clock)
• (Saat) beş**te**	**at** five (o'clock)
• (Saat) ona yirmi **kala****	**at** twenty to ten
• (Saat) onu yirmi **geçe*****	**at** ten twenty
• (Saat) dokuza beş **kala**	**at** five to nine
• (Saat) dokuzu beş **geçe**	**at** nine five

*   The word 'saat' may be omitted.
**   The origin of 'kala ' is the verb 'kalmak'
*** The origin of 'geçe ' is the verb 'geçmek'

••

EXERCISE 25
Try to say the following times in Turkish. The correct answers are on your CD. Repeat them in the gaps provided.

1. ten past five
2. ten past nine
3. five past ten
4. a quarter past eleven
5. half past eleven
6. a quarter to three
7. twenty five to five
8. five to three
9. twenty past six
10. ten to five
11. half past seven
12. twenty six past two
13. at five ten
14. at six twenty
15. at twenty to two
16. at a quarter to four
17. at half past ten

••

◆ NERE , BURA , ORA , ŞURA

neresi?	what place?
burası	this place
orası	that place
şurası	that place

■ The roots of these words are:

nere, bura, ora, şura

■ These absolute forms are not used in modern literary Turkish.

Dative Forms

nereye?	to where?
buraya	to here
oraya	to there
şuraya	to there

- **Dün nereye gittin?**   Where did you go yesterday?
- **Buraya geldiler.**   They came here.
- **Oraya gittiler**.   They went there.
- **Şuraya gitti.**   He went there.

Locative Forms

nerede?	at what place?
burada	at this place
orada	at that place
şurada	at that place

- **(Benim) kalemim nerede(dir)?**   Where is my pen?
- **Kaleminiz burada(dır).**   Your pen is here.
- **İşte, (o kalem) burada(dır).**   Here it is.
- **Kalemin orada(dır).**   Your pen is there.
- **Kalemin şurada(dır).**   Your pen is there.

- Çantam nerede?
- İşte, burada.

Ablative Forms

nere**den?**	from where?
bura**dan**	from here
ora**dan**	from there
şura**dan**	from there

- **Nereden geldiler?**   Where did they come from?
- **Londra'dan geldiler.**   They came from London.
- **Buradan gittiler.**   They went from here.
- **Oradan geldiler.**   They came from there.
- **Şuradan geldiler.**   They came from there.

♦ EXPRESSIONS OF LOCATION

İÇ : (the) inside, interior

dolap: cupboard

- **dolabın içi**   (the) inside of a cupboard
- **dolabın içinde**   in the cupboard
- **dolabın içine**   into the cupboard

♦ as an adjective: **iç kapı**   inside door

DIŞ : (the) outside, exterior

- **evin dışı**   (the) outside of a house
- **evin dışında**   outside the house

♦ as an adjective: **dış kapı**   outside door

ALT : bottom, base, under part

kutu : (the) box

- **kutunun altı**   (the) bottom of the box
- **kutunun altında**   under the box
- **kutunun altına**   under the box
- **kutunun altından** from under the box

♦ as an adjective :   **alt bölüm**   bottom part

ÜST : top, upper part, outside surface

gardırop : (the) wardrobe

- **gardırobun üstü**   (the) top of the wardrobe

- **gardırobun üstünde**   on (the) top of the wardrobe
- **gardırobun üstünden**   from the top of the wardrobe
- **Kitap masanın üstündedir.**   The book is on the table.
- **Kitabımı masanın üstüne koydum.** I put my book on the table.

◆ as an adjective :   **üst bölüm** upper part

ÜZERİ : space or place over

kent : city

- **evin üzerinden**   over the house
- **Uçak kentin üzerinden geçti.** The plane passed over the city.

ÖN : space in front, front part, foreground

evin önü   (the) front of the house

- **Evin önünde Ayşe'yi gördüm.**
  I saw Ayşe in front of the house.

- **Önümden bir araba geçti.**
  A car passed in front of me.

- **Radyoyu dolabın önüne koydum.**
  I put the radio in front of the cupboard.

◆ as an adjective :   **ön kapı**   front door

ARKA : space in back, back part, far side

- **Kutunun arkasında bir kitap gördüm.**
  I saw a book behind the box.

- **Evin arkasına kutuyu koydular.**
  They put the box behind the house.

- **Arkamdan bir araba geçti.**
  a car passed behind me.

♦ as an adjective :   **arka kapı**   back door

YAN : side, place next, vicinity of a thing

- **Merve'nin yanında, Okan'ı gördüm.**
  I saw Okan beside Merve.

- **Radyo kitabın yanındadır.**
  The radio is beside the book.

- **Sinema tiyatronun yanında(dır).**
  The cinema is next to the theatre.

- **yan yana**   side by side

- **yan etki**   side effect

ARA(SI) : middle, intermediate, space between

- **Araba aramızdan geçti.**
  The car passed between us.

- **Eskişehir, Ankara ile İstanbul arasındadır.**
  Eskişehir is between Ankara and Istanbul.

- **Kitabımı, televizyon ile radyonun arasına koydum.**
  I put my book between the television and the radio.

♦ as an adjective :   **ara yol**   middle way

CİVAR : around, nearby

- **evin civarında**   around the house

- **Okulun civarında, bazı öğrenciler gördüm.**
  I saw some students around the school.

EXERCISE 26

Look at the following sentences and listen to the CD. Repeat the sentences in the gaps provided.

1. Kitap dolabın içinde(dir)
2. Defterimi dolabın içine koydum
3. Evin dışı çok güzel
4. Masa evin dışında(dır)
5. Kutunun altı çok dar(dır)
6. Makas kutunun altında(dır)
7. Kutunun altına bakın
8. Makası kutunun altından alır mısınız?
9. Elbise gardırobun üstünde(dir)
10. Kedi gardırobun üstünden geçti
11. Kitabımı masanın üstüne koydum
12. Uçak kentin üzerinden geçti
13. Evin önünde Ayşe'yi gördüm
14. Önümden bir araba geçti
15. Radyoyu dolabın önüne koydum
16. Kutunun arkasında bir kitap gördüm
17. Evin arkasına kutuyu koydular
18. Arkamdan bir araba geçti
19. Merve'nin yanında Okan'ı gördüm
20. Radyo kitabın yanındadır
21. Sinema tiyatronun yanında(dır)
22. Araba aramızdan geçti
23. Eskişehir Ankara ile İstanbul arasındadır
24. Kitabımı televizyon ile radyonun arasına koydum
25. Okulun civarında bazı öğrenciler gördüm.

LESSON 8

◆ SIMPLE PRESENT TENSE

■ When the verb stem ends in a consonant :

Verb Stem +	Tense particle: (a/e/ı/i/ü/u)r +	Personal suffix	
gel	ir	im	I come
gel	ir	sin	you come
gel	ir		he (she, it) comes
gel	ir	iz	we come
gel	ir	siniz	you come
gel	ir	ler	they come

- alırım   I take
- bakarım   I look
- gülerim   I laugh
- görürüm   I see
- konuşurum   I speak

- Her sabah erken kalkarım.
  I get up early every morning.

- Hemşireler hastalara bakarlar.
  Nurses look after patients.

- Yüzme havuzu 9.00'da açılır.
  The swimming pool opens at 9.00.

- Dünya güneşin çevresinde dön**er**.
  The world goes round the sun.

■ When the verb stem ends in a vowel :

Verb Stem   +   r   +   Personal suffix

oku	**r**	**um**	I read
oku	**r**	**sun**	you read
oku	**r**		he (she, it) reads
oku	**r**	**uz**	we read
oku	**r**	**sunuz**	you read
oku	**r**	**lar**	they read

- yürür**üm**   I walk
- tarar**ım**   I comb
- ezberle**rim**   I memorize

- Genellikle haftada iki kez tenis oynar**ım**.
  I usually play tennis twice a week.

- Su 100 santigrat derecede kaynar.
  Water boils at 100 degrees centigrade.

- Her gün yürür**üm**.
  I walk every day.

- Sık televizyon izle**rim**.
  I often watch television.

- Her akşam kitap oku**rum**.
  I read book every evening.

Negative

Verb Stem	+ me / ma (z) +	Personal suffix	
gel	me	m	I don't come
gel	mez	sin	you don't come
gel	mez		he (she, it) doesn't come
gel	me	yiz	we don't come
gel	mez	siniz	you don't come
gel	mez	ler	they don't come

oku	ma	m	I don't read
oku	maz	sın	you don't read
oku	maz		he (she, it) doesn't read
oku	ma	yız	we don't read
oku	maz	sınız	you don't read
oku	maz	lar	they don't read

- Güneş batıda doğ**maz.**
  The sun doesn't rise in the west.

- Her akşam televizyon izle**meyiz.**
  We don't watch television every evening.

- Ben sık çay iç**mem.**
  I don't often drink tea.

- Fare kedi yakala**maz /**
- Fareler kedi yakala**maz /**
- Fareler kedileri yakala**maz /**
- Fareler kedi(leri) yakala**mazlar.**
  Mice don't catch cats.

Interrogative

mı / mi / mu / mü

gel	ir	mi	yim?	do I come?
gel	ir	mi	sin?	do you come?
gel	ir	mi ?		does he (she, it) come?
gel	ir	mi	yiz?	do we come?
gel	ir	mi	siniz?	do you come?
gel	irler	mi ?		do they come?

oku	r	mu	yum?	do I read?
oku	r	mu	sun?	do you read?
oku	r	mu?		does he(she, it) read?
oku	r	mu	yuz?	do we read?
oku	r	mu	sunuz?	do you read?
oku	rlar	mı?		do they read?

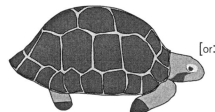

Kaplumbağa yavaş yürür
[or: Kaplumbağalar yavaş yürür(ler)]

- Ne alırsınız ?

- bakar **mıyım**?   do I look?
- yürür **müsün**?   do you walk?
- görür **müyüz**?   do we see?

- Her sabah erken kalkar **mısın**?
  Do you get up early every morning?

- Hemşireler hastalara bakarlar **mı**?
  Do nurses look after patients?

- Yüzme havuzu 9.00'da açılır **mı**?
  Does the swimming pool open at 9.00?

- Dünya güneşin çevresinde döner **mi**?
  Does the world go round the sun?

- Genellikle haftada iki kez tenis oynar **mısınız**?
  Do you usually play tennis twice a week?

- Su 100 santigrat derecede kaynar **mı**?
  Does water boil at 100 centigrade?

- Her gün yürür **müsün**?
  Do you walk every day?

- Sık televizyon izler **misiniz**?
  Do you often watch television?

- Her akşam kitap okur **mu**?
  Does she read book every evening?

- Ehliyetinizi görebilir miyim?

Negative Interrogative

mez / maz

gel	mez	mi	yim?	don't I come?
gel	mez	mi	sin?	don't you come?
gel	mez	mi ?		doesn't he (she, it) come?
gel	mez	mi	yiz?	don't we come?
gel	mez	mi	siniz?	don't you come?
gel	mez(ler)	mi ?		don't they come?

sat	maz	mı	yım?	don't I sell?
sat	maz	mı	sın?	don't you sell?
sat	maz	mı?		doesn't he sell?
sat	maz	mı	yız?	don't we sell?
sat	maz	mı	sınız?	don't you sell?
sat	maz(lar)	mı?		don't they sell?

- Her sabah erken kalk**maz mısın?**
  Don't you get up early every morning?

- Hemşireler hastalara bak**mazlar mı?**
  Don't nurses look after patients?

- Yüzme havuzu 9.00'da açıl**maz mı?**
  Doesn't the swimming pool open at 9.00?

- Dünya güneşin çevresinde dön**mez mi?**
  Doesn't the world go round the sun?

- Su 100 santigrat derecede kayna**maz mı?**
  Doesn't water boil at 100 degrees centigrade?

- Her gün yürü**mez misin?**
  Don't you walk every day?

- Sık televizyon izle**mez misiniz?**
  Don't you often watch television?

■ The verbs **'gitmek'** and **'etmek'** in the simple present tense:

The last letter **'t'** in the stems of these verbs is a variable consonant **(t/d)**.

giderim	I go
gidersin	you go
gider	he goes
gideriz	we go
gidersiniz	you go
giderler	they go
ederim	I do
edersin	you do
eder	he does
ederiz	we do
edersiniz	you do
ederler	they do

Some special uses of 'Simple Present Tense:

- **Bu akşam onu geri getiririm.**
  I'll bring it back this evening.

- **Kapıyı kapatır mısınız, lütfen?**
  Will you shut the door, please?

- **Şimdi ona telefon ederim.**
  I'll phone her now.

- **Yarın arabanızı tamir ederim.**
  I'll repair your car tomorrow.

- **Alışverişi ben yaparım.**
  I'll do the shopping.

■ gel**ir** gel**mez** - as soon as he comes:

- Kitap okumayı bitir**ir** bitir**mez**, sinemaya gideceğim.
  As soon as I finish reading book, I'll go to the cinema.

- İstanbul'a var**ır** var**maz**, onlarla konuşacağız.
  As soon as we arrive in Istanbul, we'll speak to them.

 EXERCISE 27

Try to write the following in Turkish. Then listen to the CD and check your answers.

1. I often go fishing and catch nothing.
2. You like meat.
3. Ulaş buys and sells cars.
4. We sit at the window and watch the traffic every day.
5. Do you ever sleep in class.
6. Cats catch mice.
7. Will you open the window, please?
8. I'll phone you as soon as I arrive.
9. I don't come home for lunch.
10. They don't go to work by car.

♦ SIMPLE PRESENT IN THE PAST
(GİDERDİM - I used to go / I would go)

The past general verb meaning 'used to' is formed by adding the necessary past tense form of 'to be' to the 3rd person singular, simple present.

- **(ben)** gider**dim**   I used to go, I would go
- **(sen)** gider**din**   you used to go
- **(o)** gider**di**   he/she/it used to go
- **(biz)** gider**dik**   we used to go
- **(siz)** gider**diniz**   you used to go
- **(onlar)** gider**lerdi**   they used to go

Negative:

- **(ben)** **gitmezdim**   I used not to go
- **(sen)** **gitmezdin**   you used not to go
- **(o)** **gitmezdi**   he/she/it used not to go
- **(biz)** **gitmezdik**   we used not to go
- **(siz)** **gitmezdiniz**   you used not to go
- **(onlar)** **gitmezlerdi**   they used not to go

Interrogative

- **(ben)** **gider miydim?** did I use to go?
- **(sen)** **gider miydin ?** did you used to go?
- **(o)** **gider miydi?**   did he/she/it use to go?
- **(biz)** **gider miydik?** did we use to go?
- **(siz)** **gider miydiniz?** did you use to go?
- **(onlar)** **giderler miydi?** did they use to go?

Negative Interrogative

- **(ben) gitmez miydim?**   didn't I use to go?
- **(sen) gitmez miydin?**   didn't you use to go?
- **(o) gitmez miydi?**   didn't he/she/it use to go?

- (biz) **gitmez miydik?**   didn't we use to go?
- (siz) **gitmez miydiniz?**   didn't you use to go?
- (onlar)**gitmezler miydi?**   didn't they use to go?

EXERCISE 28

Put the verbs in the brackets into 'simple present in the past'

1. (Ben) sık balığa (gitmek) ve hiçbir şey (yakalamamak)
2. (Sen) et (sevmek)
3. Ulaş araba (almak) ve (satmak)
4. (Biz)her gün pencerede (oturmak) ve trafiği (izlemek)
5. (Siz) sınıfta hiç (uyumak) ?
6. (Ben) öğle yemeği için eve (gelmemek).
7. (Onlar) işe arabayla (gitmemek)

♦ FUTURE TENSE

Future tense
particle

Verb stem + (ecek / acak) + Personal suffix

(ben)	gel	eceğ**	im	I will (am going to) come
(sen)	gel	ecek	sin	you will (are going to) come
(o)	gel	ecek		he/she/it will (is going to) come
(biz)	gel	eceğ**	iz	we will (are going to) come
(siz)	gel	ecek	siniz	you will (are going to)come
(onlar)	gel	ecek	ler	they will (are going to) come

(ben)	oku	*yacağ**	ım	I will (am going to) read
(sen)	oku	yacak	sın	you will (are going to) read
(o)	oku	yacak		he/she/it will (is going to) read
(biz)	oku	yacağ**	ız	we will (are going to) read
(siz)	oku	yacak	sınız	you will (are going to) read
(onlar)	oku	yacak	lar	they will (are going to) read

*Note that the last letter in the stem of the verb **'okumak'** is a vowel (ok**u**). The buffer **'y'** is put between two vowels.

The future tense particle is **'ecek / acak'.   **'k'** is a variable consonant (**k/ğ**).

- **yaz**mak   to write
  yaz**acağım**   I will write

- **koş**mak   to run
  koş**acaksın**   you will run

- **yürü**mek   to walk
  yürü**yecek**   he will walk

- **temizle**mek   to clean
  temizle**yeceğiz**   we will clean

- **boya**mak   to paint
  boya**yacaksınız**   you will paint

- **değiştir**mek   to change
  değiştir**ecekler**   they will change

■ There isn't any difference of translation between 'will' and 'be going to'.

> **geleceğim :   I will come** or **I'm going to come**

Negative

gel	me	Negative sign		
gel	me	*yeceğ	im	I won't come
gel	me	yecek	sin	you won't come
gel	me	yecek		he/she/it won't come
gel	me	yeceğ	iz	we won't come
gel	me	yecek	siniz	you won't come
gel	me	yecek	ler	they won't come

oku	ma	yacağ	ım	I won't read
oku	ma	yacak	sın	you won't read
oku	ma	yacak		he/she/it won't read
oku	ma	yacağ	ız	we won't read
oku	ma	yacak	sınız	you won't read
oku	ma	yacak	lar	they won't read

* **'y'** is a buffer

- **yazmayacağım**   I won't write
- **koşmayacaksın**   you won't run
- **yürümeyecek**   he won't walk
- **temizlemeyeceğiz**   we won't clean
- **boyamayacaksınız**   you won't paint
- **değiştirmeyecekler**   they won't change

Interrogative

gel	ecek	mi	yim?	will I come?
gel	ecek	mi	sin?	will you come?
gel	ecek	mi?		will he/she/it come?
gel	ecek	mi	yiz?	will we come?
gel	ecek	mi	siniz?	will you come?
gel	ecek(ler)	mi?		will they come?

oku	yacak	mı	yım?	will I read?
oku	yacak	mı	sın?	will you read?
oku	yacak	mı?		will he/she/it read?
oku	yacak	mı	yız?	will we read?
oku	yacak	mı	sınız?	will you read?
oku	yacak(lar)	mı?		will they read?

- **yazacak mıyım?**   will I write?
- **koşacak mısın?**   will you run?
- **yürüyecek mi?**   will he walk?
- **temizleyecek miyiz?**   will we clean?
- **boyayacak mısınız?**   will you paint?
- **değiştirecek(ler) mi?**   will they change?

Negative Interrogative

gel	me	yecek	mi	yim?	won't I come?
gel	me	yecek	mi	sin?	won't you come?
gel	me	yecek	mi?		won't he/she/it come?
gel	me	yecek	mi	yiz?	won't we come?
gel	me	yecek	mi	siniz?	won't you come?
gel	me	yecek(ler)	mi?		won't they come?

oku	ma	yacak	mı	yım?	won't I read?
oku	ma	yacak	mı	sın?	won't you read?
oku	ma	yacak	mı?		won't he/she/it read?
oku	ma	yacak	mı	yız?	won't we read?
oku	ma	yacak	mı	sınız?	won't you read?
oku	ma	yacak(lar)	mı?		won't they read?

- **yazmayacak mıyım?**   won't I write?
- **koşmayacak mısın?**   won't you run?
- **yürümeyecek mi?**   won't he walk?
- **temizlemeyecek miyiz?**   won't we clean?
- **boyamayacak mısınız?**   won't you paint?
- **değiştirmeyecek(ler) mi?**   won't they change?

■ The verbs 'gitmek' and 'etmek' in the future tense

The last letter 't' in the stems of these verbs is a variable consonant (**t/d**).

gideceğim	I will go
gideceksin	you will go
gidecek	he will go
gideceğiz	we will go
gideceksiniz	you will go
gidecekler	they will go

edeceğim	I will do
edeceksin	you will do
edecek	he will do
edeceğiz	we will do
edeceksiniz	you will do
edecekler	they will do

EXERCISE 29

Put the verbs in brackets into future tense and try to translate. Then listen to the CD for the correct answers and repeat them in the gaps provided.

1. Ben sizi orada (beklemek)
2. Sen gelecek yıl buraya (gelmek)
3. O evini (satmak)
4. Biz nerede (kalmak) ?
5. Siz yarın evde (kalmamak)
6. Onlar gelecek hafta yemek odasını (boyamak)
7. Biz sinemaya (gitmek).

FUTURE IN THE PAST

Third person singular, future + Past tense suffix	
(Ben) gidecek + tim	I was going to go

gidecek**tim**	I was going to go
gidecek**tin**	you were going to go
gidecek**ti**	he/she/it was going to go
gidecek**tik**	we were going to go
gidecek**tiniz**	you were going to go
gidecek**lerdi**	they were going to go

- **Bir mektup yazacaktım fakat unuttum.**
  I was going to write a letter but I forgot.

- **Futbol oynayacaktık fakat yağmur yağdı.**
  We were going to play football but it rained.

◆ PAST INDEFINITE (GİTMİŞ)

■ In the simple past tense(past definite tense):
  When you say '**o gitti** - he went', you are sure he went (it is definite).
■ In the past indefinite form:
  When you say '**o gitmiş**', it means 'he (allegedly, reportedly, presumably, unconsciously) went' but you may not be sure enough to say 'o gitti'.

verb stem	+	Past indefinite particle (mış/ miş/ muş/ müş)	+ personal suffix
(ben) git		miş	im
(sen) git		miş	sin
(o) git		miş	
(biz) git		miş	iz
(siz) git		miş	siniz
(onlar) git		miş	ler

- **yazmak** : to write

yazmışım	I (allegedly, reportedly) wrote / have written
yazmışsın	you(reportedly, allegedly) wrote / have written
yazmış	he (allegedly, reportedly) wrote / has written
yazmışız	we (allegedly, reportedly) wrote / have written
yazmışsınız	you (allegedly, reportedly) wrote / have written
yazmışlar	they (allegedly, reportedly) wrote / have written

Negative:

yazmamışım	I (allegedly, reportedly) didn't write / haven't written
yazmamışsın	you (allegedly, reportedly) didn't write / haven't written
yazmamış	he (allegedly, reportedly) didn't write / hasn't written
yazmamışız	we (allegedly, reportedly) didn't write / haven't written
yazmamışsınız	you (allegedly, reportedly) didn't write / haven't written
yazmamışlar	they (allegedly, reportedly) didn't write / haven't written

Interrogative:

yazmış mıyım?
yazmış mıyım?
yazmış mı?
yazmış mıyız?
yazmış mısınız?
yazmışlar mı?

Negative-Interrogative:

yazmamış mıyım?
yazmamış mısın?
yazmamış mı?
yazmamış mıyız?
yazmamış mısınız?
yazmamışlar mı?

■ When the indefinite particle 'miş/mış' is preceded by the third person singular and plural, simple present / present continuous:

- İyi yüzermiş (or:yüzüyormuş).
  It seems (it is said) he used to swim well.

- Okula gitmezmişim (or:gitmiyormuşum).
  It is said I used not to go to the school. (but I don't remember)

- Çok iyi İngilizce konuşurmuşsun (or:konuşuyormuşsun).
  It is said (it seems) you used to speak English very well.

- Her gün gazete okurlarmış (or:okuyorlarmış).
  It is said (it seems) they used to read newspaper every day.

- Her ay dağa tırmanırmışsınız (or:tırmanıyormuşsunuz).
  It is said (it seems) you used to climb mountains every month.

- Tatilimizi Türkiye'de geçirirmişiz (or:geçiriyormuşuz)
  It is said we used to spend our holiday in Turkey.
  (but we don't remember).

Present Indefinite

- Aslı, şimdi, Ankara'da yaşıyormuş.
  It is said that Aslı is living in Ankara.

- Müge, her sabah saat sekizde kalkarmış (or: kalkıyormuş).
  It is said that Müge gets up at 8 o'clock every morning.

Future Indefinite

- Grev, yarın başlayacakmış.
  It is said that the strike will begin tomorrow.

(Sanki) ....mış/miş gibi (as if ...):

- (Sanki) uyumamış gibi görünüyorsunuz.
  You look as if you haven't slept.

- **Bana, (sanki) deliymişim gibi baktılar.**
  They looked at me as if I was mad.

- **(Sanki) yağmur yağacakmış gibi görünüyordu.**
  It looked as if it was going to rain.

- **Ev, (sanki) içinde hiç kimse yaşamıyormuş gibi görünüyordu.**
  The house looked as if nobody was living in it.

- **Bana, (sanki) kendi oğullarıymışım gibi davranıyorlar.**
  They treat me as if I were their own son.

EXERCISE 30
Try to write in Turkish.

1. They (allegedly, reportedly) went to the party.
2. You (allegedly, reportedly) have seen that film.
3. She (allegedly, reportedly) bought a car.
4. She (allegedly, reportedly) didn't sell her car.
5. They (allegedly, reportedly) haven't painted the wall.
6. It seems (it is said) he used to run well.
7. It seems (it is said) they used to go to the cinema five times a week.
8. It seems (it is said) you used to drive very fast.
9. It seems (it is said) they used to live in Ankara.

FUTURE PERFECT TENSE

Past indefinite, 3rd person singular + Future tense of 'olmak: to be'
(Ben) gelmiş olacağım   I will have come

- **Siz oraya gidinceye kadar, dükkan kapanmış olacak.**
  By the time you get there, the shop will have closed.

- **Sen eve gelinceye kadar, ben uyumuş olacağım.**
  By the time you come home, I will have slept.

GELMİŞ OLMALI - HE MUST HAVE COME

- **gelmiş olmalıyım**   I must have come
- **gelmiş olmalısın**   you must have come
- **gelmiş olmalı**   he must have come
- **gelmiş olmalıyız**   we must have come
- **gelmiş olmalısınız**   you must have come
- **gelmiş olmalı(lar)**   they must have come

- **gelmiş olabilirim (olabilirdim)**   I might have come
- **gelmiş olabilirsin (olabilirdin)**   you might have come
- **gelmiş olabilir (olabilirdi)**   he might have come
- **gelmiş olabiliriz (olabilirdik)**   we might have come
- **gelmiş olabilirsiniz (olabilirdiniz)**   you might have come
- **gelmiş olabilir(ler) [olabilir(ler)di]** they might have come

Note also:

- **Sen Okan olmalısın.**
  You must be Okan.

- **Kitap masanın üstünde olmalı.**
  The book must be on the table.

LESSON 9

♦ QUESTIONS

■ We usually make questions by using the interrogative particle **'mı/mi/mu/mü**. The interrogative particle is followed by the personal suffix.

• okuyor **mu**yum?	am I reading?
• okuyor **mu**sun?	are you reading?
• okuyor **mu**ydunuz?	were you reading?
• okudunuz **mu**?	did you read?
• okuyacak **mı**sınız?	are you going to read?
• okuyabilir **mi**siniz?	can you read?
• gördü **mü**?	did he/she see?
• yürüdün **mü**?	did you walk?

☞ Note that 'question particle + personal suffix' is written separately.

INTERROGATIVES

• **nasıl?**	how?,
• **ne?**	what?
• **kim?**	who?
• **kaç?**	how many?, how much?
• **ne zaman?**	when?, what time?
• **nerede?**	where?
• **nereye?**	where?
• **hangi?**	which?

Study the following examples:

- **Kim** yemek için bir şey istiyor?
  Who wants something to eat?

- Radyoyu **kim** icat etti?
  Who invented the radio?

- Bu düğme bu makineyi çalıştırır **mı** ?   *(1)
  Does this switch operate this machine ?

- Bu düğme **mi** bu makineyi çalıştırıyor ? *(2)
  Does this switch operate this machine ?

- **Hangi** düğme bu makineyi çalıştırıyor?
- Bu makineyi **hangi** düğme çalıştırıyor?
  Which switch operates this machine?

- Kapıyı kilitlediniz **mi** ? *(1)
  Have you locked the door?

- Kapıyı **mı** kilitlediniz ? *(2)
  Have you locked the door?

- **Neden** kapıyı kilitlemediniz?
- Kapıyı **neden** kilitlemediniz?
  Why didn't you lock the door?

- (Onlar) gittiler **mi** ? *(1)
  Did they go ?

- Onlar **mı** gitti(ler) ? *(2)
  Did they go ?

- **Nereye** gittiler?
  Where have they gone?

- **Nerede** yaşıyorsunuz?
  Where do you live?

- Eviniz **nerede(dir)**?
  Where is your house?

- Film başladı **mı**?
  Has the film begun?

- Film **ne zaman** başlıyor?
  When does the film begin?

- Gidecek **mi**siniz?
  Are you going to go?

- **Ne zaman** gideceksiniz?
  When are you going to go?

- Saat **kaç**?
  What time is it?

- **Kaç** yaşındasınız?
  How old are you?

- O kitabı okuyor **mu**sun?   *(1)
  Are you reading that book?

- O kitabı **mı** okuyorsun?   * (2)
  Are you reading that book?

- **Hangi** kitabı okuyorsun?
  Which book are you reading?

- O kitabı okuyor **muy**dun?
  Were you reading that book?

- **Ne** yazacaktınız?
  What were you going to write?

- Mektubu yazacak **mı**ydın? *(1)
  Were you going to write the letter?

- Mektubu **mu** yazacaktın? *(2)
  Were you going to write the letter?

- Sigara içer **mi**ydiniz?
  Did you use to smoke?

- **Ne kadar sık** (or: **Ne sıklıkta**) sinemaya gidersiniz ?
  How often do you go to the cinema?

*(1) The verb of the sentence is emphasized.
*(2) The object of the sentence is emphasized.

- Affedersiniz ! Afrika'ya nasıl gidebilirim ?

 ### EXERCISE 31

Try to write in Turkish. Then listen to your CD and check
your answers.
1. Has the film begun?
2. What's Aslı doing at the moment?
3. How often do you go to the dentist?
4. Did he repair his bicycle?
5. When are you going to come to see me?
6. Why have they sold their car?
7. Which book were they going to read?

♦ AUXILIARY VERBS (YAPMAK - ETMEK)

The most common auxiliary verbs are '**etmek**' and '**yapmak**'. Both mean 'to do, doing'. They are rarely used as main verbs.

These verbs are used with numerous nouns, especially with Arabic ones.

• **gevezelik**	chattering
• **gevezelik etmek**	to chatter (to do the action 'gevezelik')
• **dua**	prayer
• **dua etmek**	to pray (to do the action 'dua')
• **teşekkür**	thanks
• **teşekkür etmek**	to thank (to do the action 'teşekkür')
• **yolculuk**	travel, travelling
• **yolculuk yapmak**	to travel (to do the action 'yolculuk')
• **hareket**	movement, act
• **hareket etmek**	to move, to act (to do the action 'hareket')

■ The cognate object is very often used in Turkish.

• **yemek**	food
• **yemek yemek**	to eat(food)
• **dikiş**	sewing
• **dikiş dikmek**	to sew(sewing)
• **yazı**	writing
• **yazı yazmak**	to write(writing)

◆ DİYE

The gerundive '**diye**' comes from the verb '**demek :** to say'.

1. It is used with direct quotations.

- **Okan " Kitabım nerede ?" diye bana sordu.**
  Okan asked me, "Where is my book?"

- **"Gelmeyeceğim" diye bağırdı.**
  He shouted "I won't come".

- **" Biz sinemaya gideceğiz" diye yanıtladım.**
  I answered "We're going to go to the cinema".

2. It means 'hoping that, on the supposition that'

- **Yağmur yağar** (or: **yağacak**) **diye dışarı çıkmadım.**
  I didn't go out, on the supposition that it would rain.

- **Türkçe çalışırız** (or: **çalışacağız**) **diye yanıma kitabımı aldım.**
  I took my book with me, hoping that we would study Turkish.

- **Arkadaşı gelir** (or: **gelecek**) **diye evde kaldı ve bekledi.**
  He stayed at home and waited on the supposition that his friend would come.

3. 'Ne diye' may be used instead of '**niçin/neden:** why'

- **Ne diye partiye gelmedin?**
  Why didn't you come to the party?

- **Paris'e ne diye gidiyorsunuz?**
  Why are you going to Paris?

◆ THE PARTICIPLE 'VERB STEM + (Y)EN / AN' (RELATIVE)

In Turkish there are not any single words equivalent to the English relative pronouns. The participles are used to express the relatives.

> **gelen adam**
> the man who is coming (comes/came/have come/had come/was coming)

- Gelen çocuk Okan'dı.
  The boy who came was Okan.

- İstanbul'da yaşayan birçok insan tanıyorum.
  I know a lot of people who live in Istanbul.

- Olan her şey benim hatamdı.
  Everything that happened was my fault.

- Kitap okuyan adam onun babasıdır.
  The man reading book is her father.

- Mutsuz sonları olan öyküleri sevmem.
  I don't like stories that have unhappy endings.

- Bu kitap evden kaçan bir kız hakkındadır.
  This book is about a girl who runs away from home.

- Polis arabamı çalan adamı yakaladı.
  The police have caught the man who stole my car.

- (Bir) vejetaryen et yemeyen kişidir.
  A vegetarian is someone who doesn't eat meat.

- Kazada yaralanan adam, hastaneye götürüldü.
  The man injured in the accident was taken to the hospital.

- Özgür ile konuşan kızı tanıyor musun?
  Do you know the girl talking to Özgür ?

- Çalan (Çalmakta olan) bir zil tarafından uyandırıldım.
  I was woken up by a bell ringing.

- Ulaş'ın, hepsi evli olan üç erkek kardeşi var.
  Ulaş has three brothers , all of whom are married.

- Note also :

  - **arabada olan adam**   or **arabadaki adam**
    the man in the car

  - **ağaçta olan kedi**   or **ağaçtaki kedi**
    the cat in the tree

  - **masada olan kalem**   or **masadaki kalem**
    the pen on the table

EXERCISE 32

Try to write in Turkish.

1. The book is about a girl who runs away from home.
2. What was the name of the horse which won the race.
3. Where are the eggs that were in the fridge?
4. A waitress who was very polite served us.
5. A dictionary is a book which gives you the meaning of words.
6. Okan's father, who is seventy-five, goes swimming every day.

◆ THE SUFFIX '--(Y) EREK / ARAK'

> **Verb Stem + '(y)erek / arak'**

When two actions happen at the same time, you can use the suffix '**...erek/arak**' for one of the verbs. The main clause usually comes second. The buffer '**y**' is used when the verb stem ends in a vowel.

- (Biz) **gülerek**, caddede yürüyorduk.
  We were walking along the street **laughing**

- **Bağırarak**, evden dışarı koştu.
  He/She ran out of the house **shouting**.

- (Ben) Kitap **okuyarak**, koltukta oturuyordum.
  I was sitting in an armchair **reading** a book.

◆ İKEN

We use '**iken(= -ken)**' when one action happens during another. It is used for the longer action. The longer action is the first part of the sentence.

> **Third person singular, simple present + ken**

- Okan, tenis **oynarken**, kolunu incitti.
- (or: Tenis **oynarken**, Okan kolunu incitti)
  Okan hurt his arm **while playing** tennis.

- Yolu **geçerken** dikkatli ol.
  Be careful when **crossing** the road.

- **Tıraş olurken**, kendimi kestim.
  I cut myself **shaving**.

- Onu, bir şey **yaparken** gördüm.
  I saw him **doing** something.

- Onu, caddede **yürürken** gördük.
  We saw him **walking** along the street.

- Kayıp çocuklar, son olarak, nehir kenarında **oynarken** görüldüler.
  The missing boys were last seen **playing** near the river.

- Onu, **dans ederken** hiç görmedim.
  I've never seen her **dancing**.

- Aslı, fırından pastaları **alırken**, kendini yaktı.
  Aslı burnt herself **as** she was **taking** the cakes out of the oven.

··

EXERCISE 33

Complete the following, using the verbs in brackets.

1. Televizyonda maç .... (izlemek), elektrik kesildi.
2. Ulaş'ı, ders ....(çalışmak), hiç görmedim.
3. Araba ....(kullanmak), çok dikkatli olun.
4. Hırsız, balkona ....(tırmanmak), polise yakalandı.
5. Sandalda balık ....(tutmak), fırtınaya yakalandık.

··

♦ ABBREVIATION (VERB STEM + [(Y) I / İ / U / Ü] P)

The suffix [**(y) ı/i/u/ü**] **p** preceded by a verb stem is used as an abbreviating device.

> **Verb Stem** + The Suffix [**(y) ı/i/u/ü**] **p**

- Dün, Okan okula gid**ip** Aslı'yı gördü.
  Okan went to the school and saw Aslı yesterday.

Note that in such a sentence 'he went and saw', the first verb receives only the abbreviating suffix, the second verb receives all the necessary suffixes.

- Ali, yerine koş**up** oturdu.
  Ali ran to his place and sat down.

Negative Form :

- Dün Okan okula gel**ip** beni görmedi.
  Yesterday Okan didn't come to school and see me.

- Geçen hafta Ankara'ya git**meyip** Bursa'ya gittim.
  Last week I didn't go to Ankara. (instead,) I went to Bursa.

■ Another abbreviating device is to use the first verb in the simple present, 3rd person singular (the personal suffixes are omitted).The last verb receives all the necessary suffixes.

- **Onlar her gün okula gelir , beni görürlerdi.**
  They would come to school each day and see me.

LESSON 10

♦ INFINITIVE AND GERUND

GELME**K , GELME**

■ When the last letter (**k**) in the infinitive is dropped out, the gerund is formed.

gelme**k** to come	**gelme**	coming	gel**me**me	not coming
gitme**k** to go	**gitme**	going	git**me**me	not going
okuma**k** to read	**okuma**	reading	oku**ma**ma	not reading
yazma**k** to write	**yazma**	writing	yaz**ma**ma	not writing

(benim)	okuma**m**	my reading
(senin)	gelme**n**	your coming
(onun)	gelmeme**si**	his/her/its not coming
(bizim)	gitme**miz**	our going
(sizin)	yürümeme**niz**	your not walking
(onların)	yazma**ları**	their writing

■ The infinitive may be used as the subject of the verb 'to be'.

- **Koşmak zor(dur).** Running is difficult.
- **Gülmek iyi(dir).** Laughing is good.

■ The verb '**istemek** - want' usually takes an infinitive as object.

- **Yürümek istiyorum.**   I want to walk.
- **Gelmek istemedi.**   He didn't want to come.

■ With the ablative suffix, the gerund refers to a negative meaning 'without .....'

- Kitabı, okuma**dan,** Aslı'ya verdim.
  I gave the book to Aslı **without** having read it.

Accusative case

- Erken kalkma**yı** severim.
  I like getting up early.

- Okuma**yı** severim.
  I like reading.

- Yürüme**yi** tercih ederim.
  I prefer walking.

- Sizin gitmeni**zi** istiyorum.
  I want you to go.

- Okan'dan bana yardım etmesi**ni** istedim
  I asked Okan to help me.

- Zengin olma**yı** isterim.
  I would like to be rich.

- Partiye gelme**yi** istiyor musun?
  Would you like to come to the party?

Dative case

- Çalışmaya devam etti.
  He continued to work.

- Bebek ağlamaya başladı.
  The baby began to cry.

- Yürümeye karar verdim.
  I decided to walk.

- Babam, arabasını (benim) kullanmama , izin verdi.
  My father allowed me to use his car.

O, erken kalkmayı sever

Kürek çekmeye başladılar

İSTEMEK - TO WANT

■ This verb also means **'to wish for, to require, to ask for, would like (to)...** etc'.

■ The verb **'istemek'** is preceded by a noun or an infinitive which is used as object.

- **Yürümek istiyorum.**
  I want to walk.

- **Televizyon izlemek istiyordum (istedim).**
  I wanted to watch television.

- **Koşmak istiyordum (istedim).**
  I wanted to run.

- **Bir fincan kahve istiyorum (rica ediyorum).**
  I would like a cup of coffee.

- **Ne yapmak istiyorsunuz?**
  What do you want to do?

- **Konuşmak istemiyorum.**
  I don't want to talk.

- **Sinemaya gitmek istemiyorum.**
  I don't want to go to the cinema.

- **Senin** (or: **senden**) **bu kitabı okumanı istiyorum.**
  I want you to read this book.

- **O, benim** (or:**benden**), **o kitabı okumamı istedi.**
  He/She wanted me to read that book.

- **Onlar, bizim**(or:**bizden**), **gitmemizi istiyorlardı.**
  They wanted us to go.

....

EXERCISE 34

Try to complete the following with the suitable suffix.

1. Spor yapma... sağlığa yararlıdır.
2. Onun gitme.... iyi oldu.
3. Sizin kalma..... gerekiyor.
4. Senin okuma... tercih ederim.
5. Benim görme.... istiyor musunuz ?
6. Saat 6.00'da gitme.... düşünüyorum.
7. Çalışma.... başladık
8. Televizyon izleme... karar verdim.

....

 ## EXERCISE 35

Write the following sentences in Turkish. Then listen to your CD and check your answers. Repeat the sentences in the gaps provided.

1. I've finished cleaning the flat.
2. Don't forget to post the letter.
3. He forgot to open the window.
4. Are you going to give up smoking?
5. Ulaş suggested going to the cinema.
6. He wanted Aslı to lend him some.
7. We have decided to go to the cinema.
8. It has started raining.
9. She promised not to be late.

....

1st Person Plural, Simple Past (gerundive)

> **1st Person plural, simple past + Possessive suffix**

(benim)	geldiğ**im**
(senin)	geldiğ**in**
(onun)	geldiğ**i**
(bizim)	geldiğ**imiz**
(sizin)	geldiğ**iniz**
(onların)	geldiğ**i** (or: geldik**leri**)

☞ Note that the words **'geldiğim, geldiğin, geldiği, ...'** are used in possessive case. The main word (gerundive) is **'geldik'** which is the 1st person plural, simple past. The last letter **'k'** is a variable consonant (k / ğ).

■ This gerundive form has three principal uses:

1. As a relative adverb:

> **O(nun) geldiği zaman**
> when he comes/came/has come

- Eve geldiğ**im zaman** (or: Eve gel**ince** / eve geldiğ**imde**), sana telefon ederim.
  When I come home, I'll call you.

- Yağmur durduğ**u zaman** (or: Yağmur dur**unca** / yağmur durduğ**unda**), dışarı çıkacağız.
  When the rain stops, we'll go out.

- Yarın Aslı'yı gördüğ**üm zaman** (or: Yarın Aslı'yı gör**ünce** /
  Yarın Aslı'yı gördüğ**ümde**), onu partiye çağıracağım.
  When I see Aslı tomorrow, I'll invite her to the party.

- Ali dersini bitirdiğ**i zaman** (or: Ali dersini bitir**ince** /
  Ali dersini bitirdiğ**inde**), bahçeye gitti.
  Ali went to the garden **when he** had finished his lesson.

- İstanbul'a geldiğ**imiz gün** (or: İstanbul'a geldiğ**imizde**) yağmur
  yağıyordu.
  The day we arrived in Istanbul, it was raining.

2. As an objective relative pronoun:

---

gördüğü adam   the man whom she sees (or: saw / has seen)

- Gördüğ**ün kadın** Pınar'ın annesidir.
  The woman whom you see is Pınar's mother.

- Kalemini aldığ**ım adam** onun babasıdır.
  The man whose pen I took is her father.

- Kaldığ**ımız otel** temiz değildi.
  The hotel where we stayed wasn't clean.

- Kaybettiğ**iniz anahtarları** buldunuz mu?
  Have you found the keys you lost?

- Okan'**ın** konuştuğ**u kızı** tanıyorum.
  I know the girl Okan is talking to.

3. With the postposition 'İÇİN'

- İşsiz olduğ**u için**, çok parası yok.
  Being unemployed, he hasn't got much money.

- Filmi, önceden iki kez gördüğ**ümüz için**, sinemaya gitmek istemedik.
  Having already seen the film twice, we didn't want to go to the cinema.

■ Accusative and Dative Cases:

- (Sen) nereye gittiğin**i biliyor musun?**
  Do you know where you are going (or: went / have gone / had gone)?

- (Onun) geldiğ**ine inanmıyorum.**
  I don't believe that he came (or: is coming / have come / had come).

- Okan'ın nereye gittiğ**ini biliyor musun?**
  Do you know where Okan is going (or: went / has gone / had gone / was going)?

- Arabamı nereye park ettiğim**i hatırlayamıyorum.**
  I can't remember where I parked (or: have parked / had parked) my car.

- (Sizin) neden güldüğünüz**ü** bana **söyleyin.**
  Tell me why you are laughing (or: have laughed / had laughed / laughed / were laughing).

- (Bizim) nasıl olduğumuz**u sordu.**
  He asked how we were.

- Ne yaptığım**ı hatırlamıyorum.**
  I don't remember what I did (have done / had done /was doing).

- Sizi tekrar gördüğüm**e sevindim.**
  I'm glad to see you again.

- (Sizin) neden gittiğiniz**e şaşırıyorum.**
  I'm surprised at why you went (or: have gone / had gone / are going / were going).

- (Onun) geldiğini gördüm.
  I saw him come / coming.

- (Sizin) koştuğunuzu gördük.
  We saw you run / running.

- Ali'nin yürüdüğünü gördü.
  He / She saw Ali walk / walking.

- Onların geldiğini(or: geldiklerini) gördüm.
  I saw them come / coming.

- Affedersiniz! Otobüs durağının nerede olduğunu söyleyebilir misiniz?
  Excuse me! Can you tell me where the bus station is?

EXERCISE 36

Complete the following with suitable form of the verbs in brackets.

1. Ben trene .... (binmek) zaman, onu gördüm.
2. Sen Ankara'da .... (olmak) yıl, hiç mektup yazmadın.
3. Onlar(ın) futbol maçına .... (gitmek) gün, ben evdeydim.
4. Benim satın almayı .... (istemek) araba çok pahalı.
5. Sizin .... (okumak) kitabı ben de okuyorum.
6. Senin böyle .... (düşünmek) inanmıyorum.
7. Sizin ne .... (demek) anlamıyorum.

♦ NECESSITY

1. THE PARTICLE 'MELİ / MALI'

■ The particle **'meli / malı'** means 'must, have to, be obliged to, ...etc'. It is attached to the verb stem and followed by the required form of 'olmak : to be'

gitmek to go	Git**meli**yim I have to go
okumak to read	Oku**malı**yım I have to read

- **(ben) yürümeliyim**   I have to walk
- **(sen) yürümelisin**   you have to walk
- **(o) yürümeli(dir)**   he/she/it has to walk
- **(biz) yürümeliyiz**   we have to walk
- **(siz) yürümelisiniz**   you have to walk
- **(onlar) yürümeli(dir)ler**   they have to walk

- **koşmalıyım**   I have to run
- **koşmalısın**   you have to run
- **koşmalı(dır)**   he has to run
- **koşmalıyız**   we have to run
- **koşmalısınız**   you have to run
- **koşmalı(dır)lar**   they have to run

Negative

(ben) git**memeli**yim   I mustn't go

- **yürümemeliyim**   I mustn't walk
- **yürümemelisin**   you mustn't walk
- **yürümemeli(dir)**   he mustn't walk
- **yürümemeliyiz**   we mustn't walk
- **yürümemelisiniz**   you mustn't walk
- **yürümemeli(dir)ler**   they mustn't walk

- **koşmamalıyım**   I mustn't run
- **koşmamalısın**   you mustn't run
- **koşmamalı**   he mustn't run
- **koşmamalıyız**   we mustn't run
- **koşmamalısınız**   you mustn't run
- **koşmamalı(dır)lar**   they mustn't run

Interrogative

- gitmeli **mi**yim?   do I have to go?
- gitmeli **mi**sin?   do you have to go?
- gitmeli **mi**(dir)?   does he have to go?
- gitmeli **mi**yiz?   do we have to go?
- gitmeli **mi**siniz?   do you have to go?
- gitmeli **mi**dirler?   do they have to go?
- gitmemeli **mi**yim?   mustn't I go?
- gitmemeli **mi**siniz?   mustn't you go?

2. ZORUNDA OLMAK (be obliged to / have to)

The required form of 'to be : olmak' is attached to the word 'zorunda' which is preceded by an infinitive.

| (Ben) gitmek **zorunda**yım | I am **obliged to (have to)** go |

- **(ben)**   gitmek zorunda**yım**   I am obliged to go
- **(sen)**   gitmek zorunda**sın**   you are obliged to go
- **(o)**   gitmek zorunda**(dır)**   he is obliged to go
- **(biz)**   gitmek zorunda**yız**   we are obliged to go
- **(siz)**   gitmek zorunda**sınız**   you are obliged to go
- **(onlar)** gitmek zorunda**(dır)lar**   they are obliged to go

Negative

- gitmek zorunda **değil**im   I don't have to go
- gitmek zorunda **değil**sin   you don't have to go
- gitmek zorunda **değil**(dir)   he doesn't have to go
- gitmek zorunda **değil**iz   we don't have to go
- gitmek zorunda **değil**siniz   you don't have to go
- gitmek zorunda **değil**(dir)ler they don't have to go

Interrogative

- gitmek zorunda **mı**yım?   do I have to go
- gitmek zorunda **mı**sınız?   do you have to go
- gitmek zorunda değil **mi**siniz? don't you have to go?

Ayşe çok çalışmak zorundadır

3. GEREK

The following forms of this word are preceded by the necessary possessive form of the gerund.

affirmative	negative
gerek	gerek **değil**
gerek**iyor**	gerek**miyor**
gerek**ir**	gerek**mez**
gerek**li**	gerekli **değil**

- Gitme**m** gerekiyor (gerek / gerekir / gerekli).
  I have to go / I should go.

- **Gitmen** gerekiyor (gerek / gerekir / gerekli).
  You have to go / You should go.
- **Gitmesi** gerekiyor (gerek / gerekir / gerekli).
  He has to go / He should go.
- **Gitmemiz** gerekiyor (gerek / gerekir / gerekli).
  We have to go / We should go.
- **Gitmeniz** gerekiyor (gerek / gerekir / gerekli).
  You have to go / You should go.
- **Gitmeleri** gerekiyor (gerek / gerekir / gerekli).
  They have to go / They should go.
- Gitmem gerek**mi**yor (gerekmez / gerekli değil).
  I don't have to go.
- Gitme**me**m gerekiyor (gerek / gerekir / gerekli).
  I shouldn't (or: mustn't) go.

-Yatmanız ve dinlenmeniz gerekiyor.

4. ...(Y)E/A GEREKSİNİMİ (or: İHTİYACI) OLMAK
(to be in need of ...)

The word 'gereksinim / ihtiyaç' is used in the possessive case.

- (Ben**im**) paraya gereksinim**im** (or: ihtiyac**ım**) var(dır).
  I need money.

- (Sen**in**) paraya gereksinim**in** (or: ihtiyac**ın**) var(dır).
  You need money.

- (**On**un) paraya gereksinim**i** (or: ihtiyac**ı**) var(dır).
  He / She needs money.

- (Biz**im**) paraya gereksinimim**iz** (or: ihtiyac**ımız**) var.
  We need money.

- (Siz**in**) paraya gereksinim**iniz** (or: ihtiyac**ınız**) var.
  You need money.

- (Onlar**ın**) paraya gereksinim**leri** (or: ihtiyaç**ları**) var
  They need money.

Negative

- (Benim) paraya gereksinimim **yok(tur)**.
  I don't need money.

- (Senin) paraya gereksinimin **yok(tur)**.
  You don't need money.

Interrogative

- (Sizin) paraya gereksiniminiz var **mı**(dır)?
  Do you need money?

- (Onun) paraya gereksinimi yok **mu**(dur)?
  Doesn't he need money?

Necessity in the past:

• yapmalı**ydım**	I had to do / I should have done
• yapmalı**ydın**	you had to do / you should have done
• yapmalı**ydı**	he had to do / he should have done
• yapmalı**ydık**	we had to do / we should have done
• yapmalı**ydınız**	you had to do / you should have done
• yapmalı**ydılar**	they had to do / they should have done
• yapma**malı**ydım	I shouldn't have done
• yapma**malı**ydın	you shouldn't have done
• yapma**malı**ydı	he shouldn't have done
• yapma**malı**ydık	we shouldn't have done

- yapma**ma**lıydınız   you shouldn't have done
- yapma**ma**lıydılar   they shouldn't have done

- yapmak zorunda**ydım**   I had to do / I should have done
- yapmak zorunda**ydın**   you had to do / you should have done
- yapmak zorunda**ydı**   he had to do / he should have done
- yapmak zorunda**ydık**   we had to do / we should have done
- yapmak zorunda**ydınız**   you had to do / you should have done
- yapmak zorunda**ydılar**   they had to do / they should have done

- yapmak zorunda **değildim**   I didn't have to do
- yapmak zorunda **değildin**   you didn't have to do
- yapmak zorunda **değildi**   he didn't have to do
- yapmak zorunda **değildik**   we didn't have to do
- yapmak zorunda **değildiniz**   you didn't have to do
- yapmak zorunda **değildiler**   they didn't have to do

- gitmem gerekiyor**du**   I had to go / I should have gone
- gitmen gerekiyor**du**   you had to go / you should have gone

- gitmem gerek**mi**yordu I didn't have to go / I shouldn't have gone
- gitmen gerek**mi**yordu you didn't have to go/you shouldn't have gone

- gitme**me**m gerekiyordu   I shouldn't have gone
- gitme**me**n gerekiyordu   you shouldn't have gone

- Düşünmen gerekiyordu !

....

EXERCISE 37

Complete the following and try to translate.

1. Şimdi git.......yim.
2. (Sen) Aslı'ya (mektup) yazma..........
3. (O) okumak için gözlük kullan.......
3. (Biz) daha hızlı yürü.............
4. (Biz) hastaneye git.......... .... ?
5. Dün (ben) erken kalk......... (in the past)
6. (Siz) partiden erken ayrılma............. (in the past)
7. (Biz) ne zaman ayrılmak zorunda...... ?
8. (Siz) çalışmak zorunda......
9. (O) neden karakola gitmek zorunda...... ? (in the past)
10.Biz.... erken ayrılma..... gerek........

....

♦ CONDITIONALS

The conditional words are 'eğer' and 'ise.
'Eğer' is the word for 'if'. It is usually omitted.
'ise' is usually used as the particle '-(y)se... / -(y)sa...'. The necessary suffixes are added to it.

(*)			Personal suffix	
(eğer) (ben)	gelir + se	+	m	if I come
(eğer) (sen)	gelir + se	+	n	if you come
(eğer) (o)	gelir + se			if he comes
(eğer) (biz)	gelir + se	+	k	if we come
(eğer) (siz)	gelir + se	+	niz	if you come
(eğer) (onlar)	gelir(ler) + se			if they come

	Personal suffix		
(eğer) gelmez + se	+	m	if I don't come
(eğer) gelmez + se	+	n	if you don't come
(eğer) gelmez + se			if he doesn't come
(eğer) gelmez + se	+	k	if we don't come
(eğer) gelmez + se	+	niz	if you don't come
(eğer) gelmez(ler) + se			if they don't come

(*) Personal pronouns may be omitted.

Type 1

A) The verb in the **if** part of the sentence:

> **Simple present or Present continuous, 3rd person singular + ise + personal suffix**

- **Kitabı bulursam, onu sana vereceğim** (or: **veririm**).
  If I find the book, I'll give it to you.

- **Kilo vermek istiyorsan, daha az ekmek yemelisin.**
  If you want to lose weight, you must eat less bread.

- **Daha az ekmek yersek, kilo veririz.**
  If we eat less bread, we lose weight.

- **Kar yağışı durursa, dışarı çıkabiliriz.**
  If it stops snowing, we can go out.

- **Telefonun çalışmıyorsa, benimkini kullanabilirsin.**
  If your telephone doesn't work, you can use mine.

- **İstersen, bu şirkette sana bir iş sağlarım.**
  If you like, I'll get a job you in this company.

- **Otobüs bekliyorsanız, kuyruğa girin.**
  If you're waiting for the bus, join the queue.

- **(Onlar)daha az ekmek <u>yerlerse</u>, kilo <u>verirler</u>.**(*)
  If they eat less bread, they lose weight.

(*) Note that the verbs are used in the 3rd person plural.

B) The verb in the **'if'** clause:

> Simple past tense, 3rd person singular + ise + personal suffix

■ In the other part of the sentence the verb is usually used in the future tense.

- **Mektubu yazdıysan, onu postalayacağım** (or: **postalayayım**)
  If you have written the letter, I'll post it (let me post it).

- **Ev ödevini bitirdiysen, televizyon izleyeceğim.**
  If you have finished your homework, I'll watch television.

Type 2

The verb in the **if** part of the sentence:

> Verb stem + ise + personal suffix

	Positive	Negative
(ben)	gelsem	gelmesem
(sen)	gelsen	gelmesen
(o)	gelse	gelmese
(biz)	gelsek	gelmesek
(siz)	gelseniz	gelmeseniz
(onlar)	gelse(ler)	gelmese(ler)

■ In the other part of the sentence the verb is usually used in 'the simple present tense' or 'simple present in the past'.

- **Bir milyon dolar kazansan, ne yaparsın** (or: **yapardın**)?
  If you won a million pounds, what would you do?

- **Bu kadar çok sigara içmese, öksürüğünden kurtulur(du).**
  If he didn't smoke so much, he would get rid of his cough.

- **Onu ziyaret etmesek, çok kızar(dı).**
If we didn't visit him, he would be very angry.

- **Çok param olsa, şu arabayı satın alabilir(d)im.**
If I had a lot of money, I could (would be able to) buy that car.

- **Saçımı kırmızıya boyasam, herkes bana güler(di).**
If I dyed my hair red, everyone would laugh at me.

- **Sigara içmeyi bıraksan, daha sağlıklı hissedebilirsin.**
(or: **hissedebilirdin**)
If you stopped smoking, you might feel healthier.

■ Keşke

Keşke gitsem   I wish I went

- **Keşke bir arabam olsa**   I wish I had a car
- **Keşke daha uzun boylu olsam**   I wish I were taller
- **Keşke odam daha büyük olsa**   I wish my room was larger

■ ....sem/sam   iyi olur - I'd better (should) .....

- **Gitsem iyi olur.**   I'd better go.
- **Gitsen iyi olur.**   You'd better go.
- **Gitse iyi olur.**   He/She'd better go.
- **Gitsek iyi olur.**   We'd better go.
- **Gitseniz iyi olur.**   You'd better go.
- **Gitseler iyi olur.**   They'd better go.

Type 3

The verb in the **if** part of the sentence:

Verb stem + ise + past tense form of 'to be'

(ben)	gelseydim	/	gelmeseydim
(sen)	gelseydin	/	gelmeseydin
(o)	gelseydi	/	gelmeseydi
(biz)	gelseydik	/	gelmeseydik
(siz)	gelseydiniz	/	gelmeseydiniz
(onlar)	gelselerdi	/	gelmeselerdi
	or: gelseydi(ler)	/or:	gelmeseydi(ler)

■ In the other part of the sentence the verb is usually used in the 'future in the past' or 'simple present in the past'.

- **Hasta olduğunu bilseydim, seni görmeye gelecektim.**
  (or: **gelirdim**)
  If I had known that you were ill, I would have come to see you.

- **Dün gece partiye gitseydin, Aslı'yı görecektin.**(or:**görürdün**)
  If you had gone to the party last night, you would have seen Aslı.

- **İşareti görseydik, durabilecektik.** (or:**durabilirdik**)
  If we had seen the signal, we could (might) have stopped.

- **Zamanımız olsaydı, müzeyi ziyaret edecektik.** (or:**ederdik**)
  If we had time, we would have visited the museum.

■ Keşke

Keşke gelseydim.　　 I wish I had come.

- **Keşke bu kadar çok yemeseydim.**
  I wish I hadn't eaten so much.

- **Keşke hava daha sıcak olsaydı.**
  I wish it had been warmer.

- **Keşke kapıyı boyamasaydım.**
  I wish I hadn't painted the door.

EXERCISE 38

A)Try to write the following in Turkish.

1. I'll go to the door if I hear the bell.
2. If it doesn't stop raining, we won't go out.
3. If you could come too, it would be very nice.
4. If the bridge broke, what would happen?
5. It would have been better if we hadn't gone.
6. He would have come if you had invited him.

B)Translate the following.

1. Beklerseniz, geleceğim (or: gelirim).
2. Bir taksi tutarsam, treni yakalayabilirim.
3. Yağmur yağsa, evde kalırız (or: kalırdık).
4. Beni çağırsalar gelirim (or: gelirdim).
5. Nehre (or: Irmağa) düşseydi, sürüklenecekti (or: sürüklenirdi).
6. Bazı haberler duymasaydım, yazmayacaktım (or: yazmazdım).

LESSON 11

♦ COMPARISON

pahalı	expensive
daha * pahalı	**more** expensive
hızlı	fast
daha hızlı	fast**er**

* 'daha pahalı' and 'daha hızlı' are comparative forms. We use the word '**daha** : more' before the adjectives.

• **ucuz**	cheap	**daha** ucuz	cheaper
• **erken**	early	**daha** erken	earlier
• **büyük**	big, large	**daha** büyük	bigger, larger
• **yavaş**	slow	**daha** yavaş	slower
• **akıllı**	intelligent	**daha** akıllı	more intelligent
• **zor**	difficult	**daha** zor	more difficult

■ The suffix '**d(t)en / d(t)an**' is used to mean English 'than'.

<u>Study the following examples:</u>

- **Daha yavaş** konuşur musunuz lütfen ?
  Could you speak **more slowly**, please ?

- **Daha sık** tenis oynardık.
  We used to play tennis **more often**.

- Buğra Ulaş'**tan** daha uzun boylu(dur).
  Buğra is taller **than** Ulaş.

- Okan Yılmaz'**dan** daha zengin(dir).
  Okan is richer **than** Yılmaz.

- Trenle yolculuk etmek, otobüsle yolculuk etmek**ten** daha ucuz(dur).
  Travelling by train is cheaper than travelling by bus.

- Sınav beklediğimiz**den** daha kolaydı.
  The examination was easier **than** we expected.

- Sandığınız**dan** daha az zamanınız var.
  You've got less time **than** you thought.

beklemek : to expect , to wait	
beklediğim**den daha**	**more** ..... **than** I expected
beklediğin**den daha**	**more** ..... **than** you expected
beklediğin**den daha**	**more** ..... **than** he/she expected
beklediğimiz**den daha**	**more** ..... **than** we expected
beklediğiniz**den daha**	**more** ..... **than** you expected
bekledikleri**nden daha**	**more** ..... **than** I expected

KADAR (as ..... as)

- Okan, Ali **kadar** zengin(dir).
  Okan is **as** rich **as** Ali.

- Yürümek, otobüsle gitmek **kadar** çabuk değil(dir)
  Walking is not **as** quick **as** taking a bus.

- Sınav, beklediğimiz **kadar** zordu.
  The examination was **as** difficult **as** we expected.

- Şafak, göründüğü **kadar** yaşlı değil(dir).
  Şafak is not **as** old **as** he looks.

... İLE AYNI (the same as ...)

- Bülent, benim**le aynı** ücreti alıyor.
  Bülent gets **the same** salary **as** me.

- Merve, Aslı'**yla aynı** yaşta(dır).
  Merve is **the same** age **as** Aslı.

- Senin saçın, benimki**yle aynı** renkte(dir).
  Your hair is **the same** colour **as** mine.

SUPERLATIVES

pahalı araba	expensive car
en pahalı araba	**the most** expensive car
kolay sınav	easy examination
en kolay sınav	**the easiest** examination

■ The adjectives are preceded by '**en**'.

• **büyük**	big	**en** büyük	the biggest
• **temiz**	clean	**en** temiz	the cleanest
• **yavaş**	slow	**en** yavaş	the slowest
• **zor**	difficult	**en** zor	the most difficult
• **iyi**	good	**en** iyi	the best
• **rahat**	comfortable	**en** rahat	the most comfortable

EXERCISE 39

Look at the following list and listen to your CD. Repeat in the gaps provided.

1. pahalı   daha pahalı   en pahalı
2. güzel   daha güzel   en güzel
3. büyük   daha büyük   en büyük
4. temiz   daha temiz   en temiz
5. zor   daha zor   en zor
6. yavaş   daha yavaş   en yavaş
7. iyi   daha iyi   en iyi
8. rahat   daha rahat   en rahat
9. kolay   daha kolay   en kolay
10.akıllı   daha akıllı   en akıllı

♦ REPORTED SPEECH

• STATEMENT

- Ben, *"bu kitabı okuyorum"* dedim. *
  I said, "I am reading this book"
- Ben o kitabı **okuduğumu** (or:**okumakta olduğumu**) söyledim.*
  I said I was reading that book.

- Ben, *"bu kitabı okudum"* dedim.
  I said, "I have read this book"
- Ben o kitabı **okuduğumu** söyledim.
  I said I had read that book.

- Sen, *"bu kitabı okuyorum"* dedin.
  You said, "I am reading this book"
- Sen o kitabı **okuduğunu** (or:**okumakta olduğunu**) söyledin.
  You said you was reading that book

- Sen, *"bu kitabı okudum"* dedin.
  You said, "I have read this book"
- Sen o kitabı **okuduğunu** söyledin.
  You said you had read that book

- Tolga, *"gazete okuyorum"* dedi.
  Tolga said, *"I'm reading the newspaper"*
- Tolga, gazete **okuduğunu** (or:**okumakta olduğunu**) söyledi.
  Tolga said he was reading the newspaper

- Orhan, *"ben bu kitabı okudum"* dedi
  Orhan said, *"I have read this book"*
- Orhan, o kitabı **okuduğunu** söyledi
  Orhan said he had read that book

- Ulaş, "Ben erken kalkarım" dedi.
  Ulaş said, *"I get up early"*
- Ulaş, erken **kalktığını** (or:**kalkmakta olduğunu**) söyledi.
  Ulaş said he got up early.

- Orhan, *"bu benim okuduğum en iyi kitaptır"* dedi
  Orhan said, *"this is the best book I've ever read."*
- Orhan, onun okuduğu en iyi kitap **olduğunu** söyledi.
  Orhan said that was the best book he had ever read.

*demek , söylemek : to say

Singular subject	Tense of the verb in the main speech	The verb in the reported speech
Ben, Sen, O	Present tense / Past tense	1st person plural, simple past (gerund) + possessive suffix + accusative suffix (geldiğ**imi**, geldiğ**ini**) *
Ben, Sen, O	Future tense	3rd person singular future (gerund) + possessive suffix + accusative suffix (geleceğ**imi**, geleceğ**ini**) *
Plural subject		
Biz, Siz, Onlar	Present tense / Past tense	1st person plural , simple past (gerund) + possessive suffix + accusative suffix (geldiğ**imizi**, geldiğ**inizi**, geldik**lerini**)
Biz, Siz Onlar	Future tense	3rd person singular future (gerund) + possessive suffix + accusative suffix (geleceğ**imizi**, geleceğ**inizi**, gelecek**lerini**)

* The last letter 'k' in the gerundive form is a variable consonant (k/ğ).

- Pınar, *"yeni bir araba **satın alacağım**"* dedi.
  Pınar said, *"I'm going to buy a new car."*

- Pınar, yeni bir araba **satın alacağını** söyledi.
  Pınar said she was going to buy a new car.

- Ulaş, *"biz **gidiyoruz**"* dedi.
  Ulaş said *"we're going".*

- Ulaş, **gitmekte olduklarını** (or:**gittiklerini**) söyledi.
  Ulaş said they were going.

- Aslı , *"biz **gittik**"* dedi.
  Aslı said *"we went / have gone".*

- Aslı, **gittiklerini** söyledi.
  Aslı said they had gone.

- Tolga, *"onlar **geldi(ler)**"* dedi.
  Tolga said 'they came / have come.'

- Tolga onlar**ın*** **geldiğini** (or: **geldiklerini**) söyledi.
  Tolga said they had come.

- Tolga, *"Aslı **geldi**"* dedi.
  Tolga said "Aslı came / has come"

- Tolga Aslı'**nın*** **geldiğini** söyledi.
  Tolga said Aslı had come.

- Buğra, *"onlar İngiltere'ye **gidecekler**"* dedi.
  Buğra said, *"they will go to England."*

- Buğra, onlar**ın*** İngiltere'ye **gideceğini** (or: **gideceklerini**) söyledi.
  Buğra said they would go to England.

*Note that the subjects '**onlar** and **Aslı** ' have possessive suffixes.

• IMPERATIVE

- Orhan, bana *"çabuk **yaz**"* dedi
  Orhan told me, *"write quickly "*
- Orhan, <u>bana</u>, çabuk yaz**mamı** <u>söyledi</u>.
  Orhan told me to write quickly.

        or:

- Orhan, <u>benden</u>, çabuk yaz**mamı** <u>istedi</u>
  Orhan asked me to write quickly.

- Tolga, sana *"dışarı **bak**"* dedi.
  Tolga told you, *"look out "*
- Tolga, <u>sana</u>, dışarı bak**manı** <u>söyledi</u>.
  Tolga told you to look out.

        or:

- Tolga, <u>senden</u>, dışarı bak**manı** <u>istedi</u>.
  Tolga asked you to look out.

- Ulaş, Buğra'ya *"piyano **çal**"* dedi.
  Ulaş told Buğra, *"play the piano "*
- Ulaş, <u>Buğra'ya</u>, piyano çal**masını** <u>söyledi</u>.
  Ulaş told Buğra to play the piano.

        or:

- Ulaş, <u>Buğra'dan</u>, piyano çal**masını** <u>istedi</u>.
  Ulaş asked Buğra to play the piano.

- Merve, bize *"kapıyı **açın**"* dedi.
  Merve told us, *"open the door. "*
- Merve, <u>bize</u>, kapıyı aç**mamızı** <u>söyledi</u>.
  Merve told us to open the door.

        or:

- Merve, <u>bizden</u>, kapıyı aç**mamızı** <u>istedi</u>.
  Merve asked us to open the door.

- Anneniz, size, *"okula **gidin"*** dedi.
  Your mother told you, *"go to school "*
- Anneniz, size, okula **gitmenizi** söyledi.
  Your mother told you to go to school.

  or:

- Anneniz, sizden, okula **gitmenizi** istedi.
  Your mother asked you to go to school.

- Özlem, onlara *"çoraplarınızı **çıkarın"*** dedi.
  Özlem told them, *"pull your socks up "*
- Özlem, <u>onlara</u>, çoraplarını çıkar**malarını** <u>söyledi</u>.
  Özlem told them to pull their socks up.

  or:

- Özlem, <u>onlardan</u>, çoraplarını çıkar**malarını** <u>istedi</u>.
  Özlem asked them to pull their socks up.

Negative:

- Tolga, sana *"dışarı **bakma"*** dedi.
  Tolga told you, *"don't look out "*
- Tolga, senden, dışarı bakma**manı** istedi.
  Tolga asked you not to look out.

- Ulaş, Buğra'ya *"piyano **çalma"*** dedi.
  Ulaş told Buğra, *"don't play the piano "*
- Ulaş, Buğra'ya, piyano çalma**masını** söyledi.
  Ulaş told Buğra not to play the piano.

• NECESSITY (MELİ / MALI)

- Emre, "gelecek hafta **gitmeliyim**" dedi.
  Emre said, *"I must go next week"*
- Emre, gelecek hafta **gitmesi gerektiğini**, söyledi

  or:

- Emre, gelecek hafta **gitmek zorunda olduğunu**, söyledi
  Emre said he would have to go the following week.

- Aslı, bana,"şimdi **gitmelisin**" dedi.
  Aslı told me, *"you must go now"*
- Aslı, bana, hemen **gitmem gerektiğini**, söyledi
  or:
- Aslı, bana, hemen **gitmek zorunda olduğumu**, söyledi
  Aslı told me I had to go at once.

- Okan, bize,"işlerinizi **bitirmelisiniz**" dedi.
  Okan told us, *"you must finish your works"*
- Okan, bize, işlerimizi **bitirmemiz gerektiğini**, söyledi
  or:
- Okan, bize, işlerimizi **bitirmek zorunda olduğumuzu**, söyledi
  Okan told us we had to finish our works.

• QUESTION

◊ **If the question has question - word:**

- Onur, bana,*"hangi kitabı **okuyorsun?**"* dedi (or: diye sordu).
  Onur asked me, *"which book are you reading?"*
- Onur, bana, hangi kitabı **okumakta olduğumu** sordu.
  Onur asked me which book I was reading.

- Öğretmen, Tolga'ya,*"adın **ne(dir)?**"* dedi (or: diye sordu).
  The teacher asked Tolga, *"what's your name?"*
- Öğretmen, Tolga'ya, adının ne olduğunu sordu.
  The teacher asked Tolga what his name was.

- Özlem, bize,*"nereye **gittiniz ?** "* dedi(or: diye sordu)..
  Özlem asked us, *"where have you gone?"*
- Özlem, bize, nereye **gittiğimizi** sordu.
  Özlem asked us where we had gone.

- Ulaş, onlara,*"ne **yapacaksınız?** "* dedi (or: diye sordu)..
  Ulaş asked them, *"what are you going to do?"*
- Ulaş, onlara, ne **yapacaklarını** sordu.
  Ulaş asked them what they were going to do.

◊ **If the question has no question - word:**

- Özben, bana,"*telefonunu kullanabilir miyim?*"diye sordu.
  Özben asked me, *"may I use your telephone?"*
- Özben, bana, telefonumu **kullanıp kullanamayacağını** sordu.
  Özben asked me if she might use my telephone.

- Özge, bize,"*sık tenis oynar mısınız?*"diye sordu.
  Özge asked us, *"do you often play tennis?"*
- Özge, bize, sık tenis **oynayıp oynamadığımızı** sordu.
  Özge asked us if we often played tennis.

- Şafak, onlara,"*Aslı'yı partinize çağırdınız mı?*"diye sordu.
  Şafak asked them, *"did you invite Aslı to your party?"*
- Şafak, onlara, Aslı'yı partilerine **çağırıp çağırmadıklarını** sordu.
  Şafak asked them if they had invited Aslı to their party.

- Özlem, Emre'ye,"*İngiltere'ye gidecek misin?*"diye sordu.
  Özlem asked Emre, *"will you go to England?"*
- Özlem, Emre'ye, İngiltere'ye **gidip gitmeyeceğini sordu.**
  Özlem asked Emre if he would go to England.

EXERCISE 40

A) Put the following into reported speech.

1. Okan, "Rusça öğrenmek   istiyorum" dedi.
   Okan, ...söyledi.
2. Yıldız, "Dün Emre'yle yolda karşılaştım" dedi.
   Yıldız, ...
3. Özben, "Damla sık dişçiye gider" dedi.
   Özben, ...
4. Tolga, "Yarın bir iş görüşmesi yapacağım" dedi.
   Tolga, ...
5. Atakan, Çetin'e "çok konuşmamalısın" dedi.
   Atakan, Çetin'e ....

B) Try to write the following in Turkish.

1. Özlem said she would answer the phone.
2. Okan said Aslı had given him a present.
3. They said they had not heard the news.
4. I told him to put it on the piano.
5. She asked me to get my hair cut.
6. We told them we had to leave at once.
7. Ulaş asked Özge what the matter was.
8. Emre asked Şafak where Aslı had put the pencil.
9. They asked if they might use the telephone.
10. Özlem asked me if I had heard a noise.

....

♦ PAST PERFECT (CONTINUOUS) TENSE

| Past indefinite, 3rd person singular + |
| Past tense form of 'to be: olmak ' |
| **gitmiştim**   I had gone, I had been going |

- **gelmiştim**   I had come, I had been coming
- **gelmiştin**   you had come
- **gelmişti**   he/she/it had come
- **gelmiştik**   we had come
- **gelmiştiniz**   you had come
- **gelmişlerdi**   they had come

- **gelmemiştim**   I hadn't come
- **gelmemiştin**   you hadn't come
- **gelmemişti**   he/she/it hadn't come
- **gelmemiştik**   we hadn't come
- **gelmemiştiniz**   you hadn't come
- **gelmemişlerdi**   they hadn't come

- **gelmiş miydim?**   had I come?
- **gelmiş miydin?**   had you come?
- **gelmiş miydi?**   had he/she/it come?
- **gelmiş miydik?**   had we come?
- **gelmiş miydiniz?**   had you come?
- **gelmiş miydi(ler)?** had they come?

- **gelmemiş miydim?**   hadn't I come?
- **gelmemiş miydin?**   hadn't you come?
- **gelmemiş miydi?**   hadn't he/she/it come?
- **gelmemiş miydik?**   hadn't we come?
- **gelmemiş miydiniz?**   hadn't you come?
- **gelmemiş miydi(ler)?** hadn't they come?

- **Partiye geldiğimde, Aslı gitmişti.**
  When I arrived at the party, Aslı had gone.

- **Ev çok kirliydi. Haftalardır temizlememiştik.**
  The house was too dirty. We hadn't cleaned it for weeks.

- **Pencereden baktığımda, yağmur yağmıştı.**
  When I looked out of the window, it had been raining.

- **Otobüs geldiğinde, 3 saat beklemiştik.**
  When the bus came, we had been waiting for 3 hours.

◆ POSTPOSITIONS

We can study the postpositions in three groups:

1. The group in which the preceding substantives have the dative suffixes.

a) RAĞMEN (KARŞIN) : despite, in spite of

- yoksulluğu**na rağmen** (or: **karşın**) **despite** his poverty
- bu**na rağmen** (or: **karşın**) **despite** this
- yürümemiz**e rağmen** (or: **karşın**) **despite** our walking

- Yağmur**a rağmen**, tatilimiz zevkli geçti.
  In spite of the rain, we enjoyed our holiday.

- Trafiğ**e rağmen**, zamanında vardık.
  In spite of the traffic, we arrived on time.

- Çok yorgun olma**ma rağmen**, uyuyamadım.
  I couldn't sleep although I was very tired.

olma**ma rağmen**
olma**na rağmen**
olma**sına rağmen**
olma**mıza rağmen**
olma**nıza rağmen**
olma**larına rağmen**

- Trafik çok kötü olma**sına rağmen**, zamanında vardık.
  Although the traffic was very bad, we arrived on time.

- Onu, önceden hiç görmememe**me rağmen**, bir fotoğraftan tanıdım.
  (or=Önceden hiç görmeme**me rağmen**, onu bir fotoğraftan tanıdım.)
  Although I had never seen him before, I recognised him from a photograph.

b) KARŞI : against, contrary, counter, opposite

- bize karşı   **against** us, **opposite** us
- karşı-etki   counter-effect

c) GÖRE : according to

- bize göre   according to us
- Orhan Doğan'a göre   according to Orhan Doğan

d) KIYASLA : in regard to, compared with

- Fiziğe kıyasla, kimya daha ilginçtir.
  Compared with physics, chemistry is more interesting

- Koşmaya kıyasla, yüzme daha iyidir.
  Compared with running, swimming is better

e) DOĞRU : straight toward

- eve doğru   straight toward the house
- arabaya doğru   straight toward the car

f) KADAR : until, up to, as far as

> **a time + ...(y)e / (y)a kadar = not later than**

- Saat sekize kadar evde olmalıyız.
  We have to be at home **by** 8 o'clock.

- Partiye gelip gelemeyeceğinizi, Pazar'a kadar söyleyin.
  Tell me **by** Sunday whether or not you can come to the party.

- Pazartesi'ye kadar geri geleceğiz.
  We'll be back **by** Monday.

- Saat on ikiye kadar çalışacağım.
  I'll be working **until** 12 o'clock.

• Saat on**a kadar**, işimizi bitirmiş olacağız.
We will have finished our work **until** 10 o'clock.

[verb stem + (y)ıncaya/(y)inceye] kadar =
by the time something happens/happened

• O gelinc**eye kadar**, konukların çoğu gitmişti.
By the time he arrived, most of the guests had left.

• Siz bu mektubu alınca**ya kadar**, ben Ankara'da olacağım.
By the time you receive this letter, I'll be in Ankara.

• İşimi bitirinc**eye kadar**, çok yoruldum.
By the time I finished my work, I was very tired.

2. The group in which the preceding substantives have the ablative suffixes :

a) ÖNCE : before

• saat yedi**den önce** — before seven o'clock
• siz**den önce** — before you, earlier than you ..
• koşma**dan önce** — before running

♦ When we use '**önce**' with the verbs :

• **gelmek** — to come
• gelme**den önce** — before coming

• **gitmek** — to go
• gitme**den önce** — before going

• **görmek** — to see
• görme**den önce** — before seeing

b) SONRA : after

- saat yedi**den sonra**   after seven o'clock
- yedi saat**ten sonra**   after seven hours
- biz**den sonra**   after us

♦ When we use '**sonra**' with the verbs:

- **gelmek**   to come
- geldik**ten sonra**   after coming

- **gitmek**   to go
- gittik**ten sonra**   after going

- **yazmak**   to write
- yazdık**tan sonra**   after writing

- **okumak**   to read
- okuduk**tan sonra**   after reading

- **yürümek**   to walk
- yürüdük**ten sonra**   after walking

- **görmek**   to see
- gördük**ten sonra**   after seeing

- **silmek**   to clean, to wipe
- sildik**ten sonra**   after cleaning (wiping)

- **satmak**   to sell
- sattık**tan sonra**   after selling

- **bağlamak**   to fasten, to tie
- bağladık**tan sonra**   after fastening

☛ Note that 'geldik, gittik,.....etc.' are the gerundive forms
(1st person plural, simple past).

c) DOLAYI : because of

- (onun) elbisesi**nden dolayı**   because of her(his) clothes
- onlar**dan dolayı**   because of them
- (sizin) gelmeniz**den dolayı**   because of your coming

d) BAŞKA : except for, apart from, other than

- siz**den** (sen**den**) **başka**   except for you
- onun kalemleri**nden başka**   apart from his (her) pens

e) BERİ : since, for

- iki saat**ten beri**   for two hours
- bin yedi yüz seksen dokuz**dan beri**   since 1789

3. In this group when the preceding substantive is a personal pronoun (except : onlar), a singular interrogative pronoun or a singular demonstrative, it requires the possessive suffix. Otherwise it is not followed by any suffixes.

a) İLE : with , by

'**ile**' is usually used as the suffix **[-(y)le / -(y)la]**

- ben(im)**le**   with me
- sen(in)**le**   with you
- on(un)**la**   with him /her / it
- biz(im)**le**   with us
- siz(in)**le**   with you
- onlar**la**   with them
- bun(un)**la** birlikte   together with this, moreover
- babası **ile**, babası**yla**   with his(her) father
- eşi **ile**,(karısı **ile**), eşi**yle**(karısı**yla**)   with his wife
- kim **ile**, kim(in)**le** ?   with whom ?
- ne **ile**, ne**yle** ?   by what ?
- tren **ile**, tren**le**   by train

■ It may also be used to mean 'and' :

- kitap **ile** kalem   (the) book and (the) pen
- Pınar **ile** Okan   Pınar and Okan
- okuma **ile** yazma   reading and writing

Baba **ile** oğul

b) GİBİ : like, similar to

- bu**nun** gibi   **like** this
- (onun) arkadaşı **gibi**   **like** his friend
- ben**im** gibi   **like** me

- Bu ev çok güzel. Bir saray **gibi.**
  This house is very nice. It's **like** a palace.

- O, ben**im** gibi, bir öğretmen.
  He's a teacher, **like** me.

- Evde herkes hasta. Evimiz bir hastane **gibi.**
  Everyone is ill at home. Our house is **like** a hospital.

The postposition 'İÇİN' : for, because of , by reason of

- bu**nun** için   because of this, for this
- ben**im** için   for me
- okumak **için**   for reading
- kadınlar **için**   for (the) women

We use the postposition **'için'** to talk about the purpose of doing something (why someone does/did/will do something).

- Bir mektup postala**mak için** dışarı çıktım.
  I went out **to** post a letter.

- Türkçe öğren**mek için** Türkiye'ye gideceğim.
  I'm going to go to Turkey **to** learn Turkish.

- Geç kalma**mak için** acele ettik.
  We hurried **so that** we wouldn't be late.

- Otobüsü kaçırma**mak için** erken ayrılın.
  Leave early **so that** you don't miss the bus.

- Yorgun hissettiğ**im için** erken yattım.
  As I was feeling tired, I went to bed early.

- Bize yakın oturduk**ları için**, onları oldukça sık görüyoruz.
  As they live near us, we see them quite often.

- İşsiz olduğ**u için**, çok parası yok.
  Be**ing** unemployed, he hasn't got much money.

- Filmi, önceden iki kez gördüğ**ümüz için**, sinemaya gitmek istemedik.
  Hav**ing** already seen the film twice, **we** didn't want to go to the cinema.

- Güzel bir gün olduğ**u için**, bir yürüyüşe gitmeye karar verdik.
  As it was a nice day, we decided to go for a walk.

- Yarın bayram olduğ**u için**, bütün dükkanlar kapalı olacak.
  As tomorrow is a public holiday, all the shops will be closed.

görmek : to see	
gör**düğüm için**	because I'm seeing/see/saw/have seen
gör**düğün(üz) için**	because you're seeing/ see/saw/have seen
gör**düğü için**	because he/she's seeing/sees/saw/has seen
gör**düğümüz için**	because we're seeing/see/saw/have seen
gör**dükleri için**	because they're seeing/see/saw/have seen

■ Çünkü - because

- Geç kaldığım için, sinemaya gitmedim.
  Because I was late, I didn't go to the cinema.
        or :
- Sinemaya gitmedim, **çünkü** geç kalmıştım.
  I didn't go to the cinema because I had been late.

...DEN BERİ, ... DİR (since ...., for .....)

■ We use both '**....den/dan beri**' and '**...dır/dir/dur/dür**' to say how long something had been happening.

- İki ay**dır** (or: iki ay**dan beri**) sigara içmiyorum.
  I haven't smoked **for** two months.

- On yıl**dır** (or: on yıl**dan beri**) İstanbul'da yaşıyorum.
  I have been living in Istanbul for ten years.

- Üç saat**tir** (or: üç saat**ten beri**) seni bekliyorum.
  I've been waiting for you for three hours.

■ We use '**...den /..dan beri**' when we say the beginning of the period.

- Kasım'**dan beri** sigara içmedim.
  I haven't smoked **since** November.

- 1987'**den beri** İstanbul'da yaşıyorum
  I have been living in Istanbul **since** 1987.

- Şubat' **tan beri** burada çalışıyor.
  She's been working here **since** February.

- Ahmet'i, Salı'**dan beri** görmedim.
  I haven't seen Ahmet **since** Tuesday.

■ We use '**...dir/dır/dür/dur**' when we say the period of time.

- Ahmet'i, üç gün**dür** görmedim.
  I haven't seen Ahmet **for** three days.

- Beş ay**dır** burada çalışıyor.
  She's been working here **for** five months.

■ Question:

Ne (kadar) zamandan beri ? or **Ne (kadar) zamandır ?** : How long?

- **Ne kadar zamandan beri** burada çalışıyorsunuz?
  How long have you been working here?

- **Ne kadar zamandır** İstanbul'da yaşıyorsunuz?
  How long have you been living in Istanbul?

USAGES OF 'AS'

English '**as**' has mainly five meanings in Turkish:

gibi, kadar, olarak, iken, için

- Bildiğiniz **gibi**, bugün onun doğum günü(dür).
  As you know, today is her birthday.

- Her zamanki **gibi** geç kaldınız.
  You are late **as** usual.

- Aslı göründüğü **kadar** yaşlı değil.
  Aslı is not **as** old **as** she looks.

- Bana, **mümkün olduğu kadar çabuk** para gönderin lütfen.
  Send me money **as soon as possible** please.

- Bir taksi şoförü **olarak** çalışıyorum.
  I work **as** a taxi driver.

- Savaş sırasında, bu oteli, bir hastane **olarak** kullandılar.
  During the war they used this hotel **as** a hospital.

- Ben ayrılır**ken**, Buğra geldi.
  Buğra arrived, **as** I left.

- Biz dışarı çıkar**ken**, yağmur yağmaya başladı.
  As we were going out, it started to rain.

- Güzel bir gün olduğ**u için**, bir yürüyüşe gitmeye karar verdik.
  As it was a nice day, we decided to go for a walk.

- Yarın bayram olduğ**u için**, bütün dükkanlar kapalı olacak.
  As tomorrow is a public holiday, all the shops will be closed.

EXERCISE 41

A) Complete the following. Then listen to your CD and check your answers.

1. Temmuz................................. Rusça öğreniyorum.
2. İki saat.................................. koşuyoruz.
3. Altı ay....................................iş arıyor.
4. Geçen yıl............................... sigara içiyorsun.

B) Try to write in Turkish. Then listen to your CD and check your answers.
1. He has been reading for two hours.
2. I have been working since 2 o'clock.
3. How long have you been playing tennis?
4. We have been waiting for her for five hours.
5. It has been raining since Saturday.

LESSON 12

◆ YAP**ABİL**MEK (TO BE ABLE / CAN / MAY)

> **Verb stem + (y)e /a + <u>bil</u> + <u>mek</u>***   : to be able to do

* **<u>bilmek</u> :** (literally)   to know (how to), to be able, to learn

■ Negative:

> **Verb stem + (y) e / (y) a + <u>me</u>mek / <u>ma</u>mak**

In The Present Continuous Tense:

yapmak to do

- **yapabiliyorum**   I can (am able to) do
- **yapabiliyorsun**   you can (are able to) do
- **yapabiliyor**   he can (is able to) do
- **yapabiliyoruz**   we can (are able to) do
- **yapabiliyorsunuz**   you can (are able to) do
- **yapabiliyorlar**   they can (are able to) do

- **yapamıyorum**   I can't (am not able to) do
- **yapamıyorsun**   you can't (are not able to)do
- **yapamıyor**   he can't (is not able to) do
- **yapamıyoruz**   we can't (are not able to) do
- **yapamıyorsunuz**   you can't (are not able to) do
- **yapamıyorlar**   they can't (are not able to) do

Interrogative:

- **yapabiliyor muyum?**   can I do?
- **yapabiliyor musun?**   can you do?

- **yapamıyor muyum?**   can't I do?
- **yapamıyor musun?**   can't you do?

In The Simple Past Tense:

gelmek to come

- **gelebildim**   I was able (= managed) to come,
                      I have been able to come
- **gelebildin**   you were able to come
- **gelebildi**   he was able to come
- **gelebildik**   we were able to come
- **gelebildiniz**   you were able to come
- **gelebildiler**   they were able to come

- **gelemedim**   I wasn't able to come
- **gelemedin**   you weren't able to come
- **gelemedi**   he wasn't able to come
- **gelemedik**   we weren't able to come
- **gelemediniz**   you weren't able to come
- **gelemediler**   they weren't able to come

- **gelebildim mi?**   was I able to come?
- **gelebildin mi?**   were you able to come?

- **gelemedim mi?**   wasn't I able to come?
- **gelemedin mi?**   weren't you able to come?

In The Simple Present Tense:

In the simple present tense we may also use it to talk about the possible happenings or possible actions in the future and to ask for permission.

gitmek to go

- **gidebilirim**   I can go, I am able to go, I may go
- **gidebilirsin**   you can go
- **gidebilir**   he can go
- **gidebiliriz**   we can go
- **gidebilirsiniz**   you can go
- **gidebilirler**   they can go

- **gidemem**   I can't go, I am not able to go (*)
- **gidemezsin**   you can't go
- **gidemez**   he can't go
- **gidemeyiz**   we can't go
- **gidemezsiniz**   you can't go
- **gidemezler**   they can't go

- **gidebilir miyim?**   can I go, may I go?
- **gidebilir misin?**   can you go?

- **gidemez miyim?**   can't I go?
- **gidemez misin?**   can't you go?

(*)The negative sentences above don't express possibility.

■ **To express the negative possibility :**

- **gidemeyebilirim**   I may not be able to go
- **gidemeyebilirsin**   you may not be able to go
- **gidemeyebilir**   he may not be able to go
- **gidemeyebiliriz**   we may not be able to go
- **gidemeyebilirsiniz**   you may not be able to go
- **gidemeyebilirler**   they may not be able to go

- Affedersiniz!
  Gazetenizi alabilir miyim?

- Teşekkür ederim.

• In The Past Continuous Tense:

koşmak   to run

- **koşabiliyordum**   I was being able to run, I could run,
  I used to be able to run
- **koşabiliyordun**   you were being able to run
- **koşabiliyordu**   he was being able to run
- **koşabiliyorduk**   we were being able to run
- **koşabiliyordunuz** you were being able to run
- **koşabiliyorlardı**   they were being able to run

- **koşamıyordum**   I wasn't being able to run, I couldn't run,
                                          I didn't use to be able to run
- **koşamıyordun**   you weren't being able to run
- **koşamıyordu**   he wasn't being able to run
- **koşamıyorduk**   we weren't being able to run
- **koşamıyordunuz**   you weren't being able to run
- **koşamıyorlardı**   they weren't being able to run

- **koşabiliyor muydum?**   was I being able to run?
- **koşabiliyor muydun?**   were you being able to run?

- **koşamıyor muydum?**   wasn't I being able to run?
- **koşamıyor muydun?**   weren't you being able to run?

In 'The Simple Present in the Past':

yürümek   to walk

- **yürüyebilirdim**   I could walk, I used to be able to walk
                                      I might have walked (*)
- **yürüyebilirdin**   you could walk
- **yürüyebilirdi**   he could walk
- **yürüyebilirdik**   we could walk
- **yürüyebilirdiniz**   you could walk
- **yürüyebilirlerdi**   they could walk

- **yürüyemezdim**   I couldn't walk, I didn't use to be able to walk
- **yürüyemezdin**   you couldn't walk
- **yürüyemezdi**   he couldn't walk
- **yürüyemezdik**   we couldn't walk
- **yürüyemezdiniz**   you couldn't walk
- **yürüyemezlerdi**   they couldn't walk

- **yürüyebilir miydim?**   could I walk?
- **yürüyebilir miydin?**   could you walk?

- **yürüyemez miydim?**   couldn't I walk?
- **yürüyemez miydin?**   couldn't you walk?

(*)The positive verb may also express the possibility.

☞ Note also:

• **Yürümüş olabilir**   He might have walked

In The Past Indefinite:

yazmak to write

• **yazabilmişim**   I (allegedly, reportedly) was able to write /
                        I (allegedly, reportedly) have been able to write
• **yazabilmişsin**   you (allegedly, reportedly) were able to write
• **yazabilmiş**   he (allegedly, reportedly) was able to write
• **yazabilmişiz**   we (allegedly, reportedly) were able to write
• **yazabilmişsiniz**   you (allegedly, reportedly) were able to write
• **yazabilmişler**   they (allegedly, reportedly) were able to write

• **yazamamışım**   I (allegedly, reportedly) wasn't able to write /
                        I (allegedly, reportedly) have been able to write
• **yazamamışsin**   you (allegedly, reportedly) weren't able to write
• **yazamamış**   he (allegedly, reportedly) wasn't able to write
• **yazamamışız**   we (allegedly, reportedly) weren't able to write
• **yazamamışsınız**   you (allegedly, reportedly) weren't able to write
• **yazamamışlar**   they (allegedly, reportedly) weren't able to write

• **yazabilmiş miyim?**   was I (allegedly, reportedly) able to write?
• **yazabilmiş misin?**   were you (allegedly, reportedly) able to write?

• **yazamamış mıyım?**   wasn't I (allegedly, reportedly) able to write?
• **yazamamış mısın?**   weren't you(allegedly, reportedly) able to write?

• **yazabilirmişim**   It is said I used to be able to write
• **yazabilirmişsin**   It is said you used to be able to write
• **yazabilirmiş**   It is said he used to be able to write
• **yazabilirmişiz**   It is said we used to be able to write
• **yazabilirmişsiniz**   It is said you used to be able to write
• **yazabilirlermiş**   It is said they used to be able to write

- **yazamazmışım**   It is said I didn't use to be able to write
- **yazamazmışsın**   It is said you didn't use to be able to write
- **yazamazmış**   It is said he didn't use to be able to write
- **yazamazmışız**   It is said we didn't use to be able to write
- **yazamazmışsınız**   It is said you didn't use to be able to write
- **yazamazlarmış**   It is said they didn't use to be able to write

• <u>In The Future Tense:</u>

görmek to see

- **görebileceğim**   I will (am going to) be able to see
- **görebileceksin**   you will be able to see
- **görebilecek**   he will be able to see
- **görebileceğiz**   we will be able to see
- **görebileceksiniz**   you will be able to see
- **görebilecekler**   they will be able to see

- **göremeyeceğim**   I won't (am not going to) be able to see
- **göremeyeceksin**   you won't be able to see
- **göremeyecek**   he won't be able to see
- **göremeyeceğiz**   we won't be able to see
- **göremeyeceksiniz**   you won't be able to see
- **göremeyecekler**   they won't be able to see

- **görebilecek miyim?** will I be able to see?
- **görebilecek misin?** will you be able to see?

- **göremeyecek miyim?** won't I be able to see?
- **göremeyecek misin?** won't you be able to see?

■ ÇOK FAZLA, AŞIRI - TOO (EXCESS)

> • Bu problem **çok** zor.
> This problem is **very** difficult.
>
> • Bu problem **aşırı** (**çok fazla**) zor. Onu çözemem.
> This problem is **too** difficult. I can't solve it.
>   or:
> • Bu problem (ben**im**)* çözemeyeceğ**im*** **kadar** zor
> This problem is **too** difficult **for me** to solve.

* **-im** : possessive suffix , **çözemeyecek :** gerundive

Verb stem + (y) amayacak / emeyecek kadar

• Okul (ben**im**) yürüyemeyeceğ**im*** **kadar** uzak.
(Okul çok fazla uzak. Oraya yürüyemem.)
The school is too far for me to walk.

• Okul (sen**in**) yürüyemeyeceğ**in*** **kadar** uzak.
The school is too far for you to walk.

• Okul (o**nun**) yürüyemeyeceğ**i*** **kadar** uzak.
The school is too far for him to walk.

• Okul (biz**im**) yürüyemeyeceğ**imiz*** **kadar** uzak.
The school is too far for us to walk.

• Okul (siz**in**) yürüyemeyeceğ**iniz*** **kadar** uzak.
The school is too far for you to walk.

• Okul (onlar**ın**) yürüyemeyecek**leri*** **kadar** uzak.
The school is too far for them to walk.

(*) Note that 'yürüyemeyeceğim(iz), yürüyemeyeceğin(iz), yürüyemeyeceği, yürüyemeyecekleri' are the possessive forms of the gerundive '**yürüyemeyecek** : he/she will not be able to walk '.

☛ Note also:

- Okul (benim) <u>yürüyebileceğ**im**</u>** **kadar** yakın.
  The school is near enough for me to walk.

- Bu problem (senin) <u>çözebileceğ**in**</u>** **kadar** kolay.
  This problem is easy enough for you to solve.

(**) Note that 'yürüyebileceğim(iz), yürüyebileceğin(iz), yürüyebileceği, yürüyebilecekleri' are the possessive forms of '**yürüyebilecek** : he/she will be able to walk '.

 EXERCISE 42

Complete the following, using the suitable forms of the verbs in brackets.

1. Ben şimdi onları .... (görmek)
   (I can see them now)
2. Sen şimdi onları ....(görmek)?
   (Can you see them now?)
3. Sonunda, Ulaş Buğra'yı ....(yenmek)
   (In the end Ulaş was able to beat Buğra)
4. Yangın çabuk yayıldı fakat biz ....(kaçmak)
   (The fire spread quickly but we were able to escape)
5. Biz bu dağın zirvesine .... (tırmanmak)
   (We can climb to the top of this mountain.)
6. Siz uzun süre .... (beklemek)
   (You may wait long)
7. Okan, daha gençken, ağaca ....(tırmanmak)
   (Okan could climb trees when he was younger.)
8. O, birkaç yıl önce, piyano .... (çalmak)
   (It is said she used to be able to play piano a few years ago)
9. Bu çorba, ... (içmek) kadar sıcak
   (This soup is too hot for me to drink)
10. Hava, dışarı .... (gitmek) kadar soğuk
   (It's too cold for us to go out)

♦ CAUSATIVE VERBS

Dün çatıyı tamir ettirdim I had the roof repaired yesterday.
Ona çatıyı tamir ettirttim. I made him repair the roof.

■ Verbs whose stems end in a consonant form the causative by adding the particle '(d/t)ir/ır/ür/ur - (t)' to the verb stem.

■ In a causative a person does not perform an action directly. When you add the letter - (t) to the particle, it indicates that the person causes it to happen by forcing another person to do it.

tamir etmek to repair :

- Dün arabayı tamir ettirdim.
  I had the car repaired yesterday.

- Yarın arabamı tamir ettireceğim.
  I'm going to have my car repaired tomorrow.

- Ona arabayı tamir ettirttim.
  I made him repair the car.

kesmek to cut :

- Saçımı kestireceğim.
  I'm going to have my hair cut.

- Ayda bir kez saçımı kestiririm.
  I have my hair cut once a month.

kırmak   to break :

- Tom, bir kavgada, burnunu kır**dır**dı.
  Tom had his nose broken in a fight.

çalmak   to steal **:**

- Ali, trende, parasını çal**dır**dı.
  Ali had his money stolen on the train.

dans etmek   to dance :

- Müzik, beni, dans et**tir**ir.
  Music makes me dance.

almak   to take :

- Annesi, ona, ilacını al**dır**ttı.
  His mother made him take his medicine.

gülmek   to laugh :

- O, bizi, gül**dür**ttü.
  He made us laugh.

■ Verbs whose stems end in a vowel form the causative by adding
' **t** ' or '**(t)tir/tır/tür/tur** '.   When you use **(t)tir/tır/tür/tur**, the
causative verb has more force and authority.

boyamak   to paint :

- Evi, kıştan önce boya**t**mak istiyorum.
  I want to get the house painted before winter.

- Evi, ona boya**ttır**dım.
  I made him paint the house.

- Şu anda evi boya**t**ıyoruz.
  We are having the house painted at the moment.

■ Some exceptions:

- **demek**   to say
- de**dirt**mek   to make someone say

- **yemek**   to eat
- ye**dir**mek   to cause to eat, to feed
- ye**dirt**mek   to make someone eat

- **doldurmak**   to fill
- doldur**t**mak to have something filled

- **oturmak**   to sit down
- otur**t**mak   to cause someone to sit down

···

EXERCISE 43

Complete the following, using the suitable forms of the verbs in brackets.

1. Dün, arabamı……………..... (yıkamak).
   (I had my car washed yesterday)
2. Ayakkabılarımı her gün ……………….. (temizlemek)
   (I have my shoes cleaned every day)
3. Okan,şu anda, saçını ………………….. (kesmek) .
   (Okan is having his hair cut at the moment)
4. Fotoğrafımı ……………….. (çekmek).
   (I am going to have my photograph taken)
5. Dün, ona, o ağacı …………………….. (kesmek)
   (I made him cut down that tree yesterday)
6. Ona, arabayı …………….. (boyamak).
   (We made him paint the car)

···

♦ PASSIVE VERBS

1) Verbs whose stems end in a consonant (other than **-l**) form the passive by adding '**ıl/il/ul/ül**' to the verb stem.

yapmak	to do	yapılmak	to be done
vermek	to give	verilmek	to be given
sunmak	to present	sunulmak	to be presented
görmek	to see	görülmek	to be seen

yapılmamak	not to be done
verilmemek	not to be given
sunulmamak	not to be presented
görülmemek	not to be seen

- **Bu ev 1815'te (bin sekiz yüz on beşte) yapıldı.**
  This house was built in 1815.

- **Aslı Amerika'ya gönderilecek.**
  Aslı will be sent to America.

- **Problem çözülüyor.**
  The problem is being solved.

- **O dün görüldü.**
  He was seen yesterday.

2) Verbs whose stems end in '**-l**' form the passive by adding '**ın/in/un/ün**'.

almak	to take, to receive	alınmak	to be taken, to be received
silmek	to clean, to erase	silinmek	to be cleaned, to be erased
bulmak	to find	bulunmak	to be found
gülmek	to laugh	gülünmek	to be laughed

alınmamak	not to be taken, not to be received
silinmemek	not to be cleaned, not to be erased
bulunmamak	not to be found
gülünmemek	not to be laughed

- **çalmak** — to steal
- **çalınmak** — to be stolen
- **çalınmamak** — not to be stolen

- **satın almak** — to buy
- **satın alınmak** — to be bought
- **satın alınmamak** — not to be bought

- **Arabam çalındı.**
  My car was stolen.

- **O kitaplar, satın alındı(lar).**
  Those books were bought.

- **Tahta, Ali tarafından silindi.**
  The blackboard has been cleaned by Ali.

- **Mektup, bizim tarafımızdan alındı.**
  The letter has been received by us.

- **Ona, herkes tarafından gülünüyor.**
  He is being laughed at by everybody.

3) Verbs whose stems end in a vowel form the passive by adding **'n'**.

- **kapamak** — to close, to shut
- kapanmak — to be closed, to be shut

- **başlamak** — to begin
- başlanmak — to be begun

- **söylemek** — to say
- söylenmek — to be said

- **kazımak**   to scrape off
- kazınmak   to be scraped off

- **temizlemek**   to clean
- temizlenmek   to be cleaned

- **okumak**   to read
- okunmak   to be read

- **beklemek**   to wait , to expect
- beklenmek   to be waited, to be expected

- **Pencereler temizlendi.**
  The windows have been cleaned.

- **İki adam, polis tarafından tutuklandı.**
  Two men were arrested by the police.

- **Biz izleniyorduk. (or: Biz takip ediliyorduk.)**
  We were being followed.

- **Bu kitap okunmalı.**
  This book should be read.

- **Onun, Antalya'da yaşadığı söyleniyor.**
  It is said that he/she is living in Antalya.

- **Grevin, yarın başlaması bekleniyor.**
  It is expected that the strike will begin tomorrow.

Bay Türker, öğrencileri tarafından çok sevilir

■ The word **'taraf'** is used in

| a possessive construction + ablative | to show the agent.

- **(benim) tarafımdan**   by me
- **(senin) tarafından**   by you
- **(onun) tarafından**   by him/her
- **(bizim) tarafımızdan**   by us
- **(sizin) tarafınızdan**   by you
- **onların tarafından**   by them

■ The agent is usually used between the noun and the verb.

Bir iş toplantısı yapılıyor

- **O gazete (birçok insan tarafından) okunur.**
  That newspaper is read (by a lot of people).

- **Arabam (tamirci tarafından) tamir ediliyor.**
  My car is being repaired (by the repairman).

- **Amerika, (Kolombo tarafından) keşfedildi.**
  (keşfetmek : to discover)
  America was discovered (by Columbus)

- **Bütün pencereler (onlar tarafından) temizlendi.**
  All the windows were (have been) cleaned by them.

- **Saatim (sizin tarafınızdan) bulunmuştu.**
  My watch had been found (by you).

- **Gelecek yıl, (onlar tarafından) yeni bir fabrika yapılacak.**
  A new factory will be built next year (by them).

EXERCISE 44

A) Complete the following sentences in the tense suggested, using the passive forms of the verbs in brackets and try to translate.

Example:
Bu alıştırma çok dikkatli .... (yapmak). - present continuous
Bu alıştırma çok dikkatli yapılıyor.
This exercise is being done very carefully.

1. Köprü geçen yıl .... (yapmak). - past
2. Pencere .... (açmak). - present continuous
3. Sorunuz .... (yanıtlamak). - future
4. Bu resme her zaman hayran .... (olmak). - simple present
5. Kitap gelecek ay .... (bitirmek). - future

B) Put the following sentences into the passive voice:

Example:
Active   : Birisi bana bir kitap verdi. (Someone gave me a book)
Passive : Bana bir kitap verildi.

1. Kız kardeşime de bir bilet verdiler.
   (They gave my sister a ticket too)
2. Bize, çeşitli sorular soruyorlar.
   (They are asking us several questions)
3. Birisi, size, trenin ne zaman kalktığını söyleyecek.
   (Someone will tell you when the train leaves)
4. Birisi işi bitirmeli.
   (Someone must finish the work)
5. Yarın, onu hastaneye götürecekler.
   (They will take her to the hospital)

LESSON 13

♦ THE SUFFIX ' --CA / CE / ÇA / ÇE'

This suffix has four principal uses:

1)
- **çocuk**   child
- çocuk**ça**   childishly, like a child

- **aptal**   stupid
- aptal**ca**   stupidly

- **akıllı**   clever, reasonable
- akıllı**ca**   reasonably

- **hoş**   pleasant, agreeable
- hoş**ça**   pleasantly, agreeably

- **soğuk**   cold
- soğuk**ça**   rather cold

- **Türk**çe   the Turkish language
- **İngiliz**ce   the English language
- **Rus**ça   the Russian language

2)
- **ben**   I
- ben**ce**   as I see it, in my opinion

- **sen**   you
- sen**ce**   as you see it, in your opinion

3) After the plural suffix :

- **on**   ten
- on<u>lar</u>**ca**   tens and tens

- **bin**   thousand
- bin<u>ler</u>**ce**   thousands and thousands

- **yüzyıl**   century
- yüzyıl<u>lar</u>**ca**   centuries and centuries

4)

Simple past, 1st person plural   + c(ç)e / c(ç)a

■ This form expresses the ideas of 'whenever', 'as long as'.

- Bebek, ona bak**tıkça,** ağladı.
  Whenever she looked at it, the baby wept.

- Dikkatli sür**dükçe** (dikkatli sür**düğün sürece**), arabamı kullanabilirsin.
  You can use my car, as long as you drive carefully.

■ **Negative:**

- Sen bağır**madıkça** (sen bağır**mazsan**), ben duyamam
  I can't hear unless you shout.

- Çok fazla ses yap**madıkça** (çok fazla ses yap**mazsa**), çocuk burada kalabilir.
  The child can stay here providing she doesn't make too much noise.

■ <u>'**gittikçe** - gradually'</u>:

- **Gittikçe şişmanlıyorsun.**
  You are gradually growing fat.

◆ ÖYLE (SO)

1) öyle=öylesine=o kadar

- **Öyle (=Öylesine / O kadar)** yorgunum ki .....
  I'm **so** tired that .....

- **Öyle (=Öylesine / O kadar)** güzel bir hava ki ......
  It's **such** lovely weather that .....

- **O kadar (=Öylesine / Öyle)** yavaş yürüme.
  Don't walk **so** slowly.

- (Onun), **O kadar (=Öylesine / Öyle)** yaşlı olduğunu fark
  etmedim.
  I didn't realize he was **so** old.

- Onu, **o kadar (=öylesine / öyle)** uzun bir süredir görmedik ki ...
  We haven't seen him for **so** long that ...

2)

  -**(Kendimi) yorgun hissediyorum.**   I'm feeling tired.
- -Ben de **öyle.**   **So** am I.

  -**Onun adını hatırlayamıyorum.** I can't remember her name.
- -Ben de **öyle.**   **Neither** can I.

- Sanırım **öyle.**   I think **so.**
- **Öyle** umarım.   I hope **so.**

♦ HÂLÂ - ARTIK (STILL - ANYMORE)

■ We use **'hâlâ'** to say that a situation or action is continuing. It is the word for 'still'.

- **Hâlâ aynı evde oturuyoruz.**
  We're still living in the same house.

- **Ahmet hâlâ işsiz.**
  Ahmet is still unemployed.

- **Ayşe hâlâ bana yazmadı.**
  Ayşe still hasn't written to me.

■ We use **'artık:** no longer, any longer**'** to say that a situation has changed.

- **Bay Okçu artık burada çalışmıyor.**
  Mr. Okçu doesn't work here any more / any longer.

- **Biz artık arkadaş değiliz.**
  We are no longer friends.

♦ BİLE - DAHA DA

■ We use **'bile** or **daha da** (or = **daha bile**)**'** to say that something is unusual or surprising. They are used to mean 'even'.

- **En iyi arkadaşı bile, ona borç vermezdi.**
- (or: **Ona, en iyi arkadaşı bile, borç vermezdi.**)
  Even his best friend wouldn't lend him.

- **Çok zengin bir ülke. En fakir insanların bile arabası var.**
  It's a very rich country. Even the poorest people own cars.

- **Aslı bütün dünyayı gezdi. Antarktika'da bile bulundu.**
  Aslı has travelled all over the world. She has even been to Antarctic.

- **Yatakta bile kravat takar.**
  He even wears in the bed.

- **Kızgın olduğum zaman bile, hiç bağırmam.**
  I never shout, even when I'm angry.

- **Seni yarın görmesem bile, hafta sonundan önce kesinlikle görüşürüz.**
  Even I don't see you tomorrow, we're sure to see each other before the week-end.

- **Dün çok sıcaktı ancak bugün daha da (=daha bile) sıcak.**
  It was very hot yesterday but today it's even hotter.

- **Ben saat beşte kalktım fakat Ayşe daha da (= daha bile) erken kalktı.**
  I got up at 5 o'clock but Ayşe got up even earlier.

◆ BÜTÜN, HEPSİ, HEPİMİZ, ÇOĞU

- **Bütün** arabaların tekerleği vardır.
  All cars have wheels.

- Bunların **hepsi** benim(dir).
  All of these are mine.

- Arkadaşlarımın **çoğu**, İstanbul'da yaşar.
  Most of my friends live in Istanbul.

- Bugün, **bütün yediğim** bir sandviç(tir).
  All I've eaten today is a sandwich.

- **Bütün** kitabı okudum.
  I've read **all** the book.

- **Bütün** yaşamını Hindistan'da geçirdi.
  He spent **all** his life in India.

- Bütün **haftayı plajda geçirdi.**
  She spent **all** week on the beach.

- **Hepimiz**, yemekten sonra, hastalandık.
  We all felt ill after the meal.

(bizim) hepimiz	we all, all of us
(sizin) hepiniz	you all, all of you
(onların) hepsi	they all, all of them

♦ BİR ŞEY, BİR YER, BİRİ(Sİ) , KİMSE

- Gözümde **bir şey** var.
  I've got **something** in my eye.

- **Biri(si)** gelebilir.
  Anybody may come.

- **Biri(si)** sizi görmek istiyor.
  Someone wants to see you.

- **Bir şeye** ihtiyacınız varsa, yalnızca isteyin (yeter).
  If you need **anything**, just ask.

- Doğum günü hediyen için, istediğin **(herhangi) bir şeyi** alabilirsin.
  You can have **anything** you want for your birthday present.

- Tatilimde **(herhangi) bir yere** gitmek istiyorum.
  I want to go **anywhere** during my holiday.

- Onlar**dan biri(si)** geldi.
  One of them came.

- İstediğiniz **(herhangi) bir şarkıyı** söyleyebilirsiniz. Benim için fark etmez.
  You can sing **any song** you want. I don't mind.

- **Kimse** var mı?
  Is **anybody** there?

- Sorusu olan **biri(si)** varsa, yanıtlayabilirim.
  If **anyone** has any questions, I can answer.

- **Kimse**nin sorusu yoksa, gidebilirim.
  If **anyone** has not any questions, I can go.

- **Biri(si)** kahvesini halıya döktü.
  Someone has spilt his/her coffee on the carpet.

◆ **HİÇ , (HER) İKİ ..... DE , NE .... NE (DE) ... , HEM ..... HEM DE... , YA....YA DA....**

- **HİÇ**

1. It is used to mean '**ever, never**, or **any**'

- **Hiç** İstanbul'da bulundunuz mu?
  Have you **ever** been to Istanbul?

- İstanbul'da **hiç** bulundunuz mu?
  Have you **ever** been to Istanbul?

- **Hiç** otobüsle yolculuk ettiniz mi?
  Have you **ever** travelled by bus?

- Otobüsle **hiç** yolculuk ettiniz mi?
  Have you **ever** travelled by bus?

- **Hiç** otobüsle yolculuk etmedim.
  I have **never** travelled by bus.

- Otobüsle **hiç** yolculuk etmedim.
  I have **never** travelled by bus.

- Orada **hiç** kitap gördün mü?
  Have you seen **any** books there ?

- **Hiç** arkadaşım yok.
  I don't have **any** friends(at all).

2. It is used to mean **'at all'**

- **Hiç** mutlu değilim.   I'm not happy **at all.**
- **Hiç** hoşnut değilim.   I'm not pleased **at all.**

- **Hiçbir şey** görmedim.   I didn't see **anything.**
- **Hiçbir şey** demedik.   We didn't say **anything.**

Study the following examples :

- (Onların) **hiç** çocukları yok.
  They don't have **any** children.

- Dolapta **hiç** peynir var mı?
  Is there **any** cheese in the fridge?

- **Hiç** açık dükkan yok.
  There are **no** shops open.

- Arkadaşlarımın **hiçbiri(si)** İstanbul'da yaşamıyor.
  None of my friends live in Istanbul.

- (Onların) **hiçbiri(si)** gelmedi.
  None of them came.

- Bunların **hiçbiri(si)** benim değil.
  None of these are mine.

(bizim) hiçbirimiz	none of us.
(sizin) hiçbiriniz	none of you
(onların/bunların) hiçbiri(si)	none of them/these

- **(Hiç) kimse** telefon etmedi
  Nobody telephoned.

- **(Hiç) kimse** beni ziyaret etmeye gelmedi. /
  Beni ziyaret etmeye **(hiç) kimse** gelmedi.
  No-one came to visit me.

- **(Hiç) kimseyi** görmedim.
  I haven't seen **anybody**.

- **(Hiç) kimse** onu gördü mü? / Onu **(hiç) kimse** gördü mü?
  Has **anybody** seen it?

- **Hiçbir şey** yapmadım.
  I did **nothing.**

- **Hiçbir yere** gitmiyorum.
  I'm going **nowhere.**

• (HER) İKİ ..... DE, (HER) İKİSİ DE

- **(Her) iki** restoran **da** çok iyi(dir).
  Both restaurants are very good.

- **(Her) iki** restoran **da** pahalı **değil**(dir)
  Neither restaurant is expensive.

- **(Her) iki** restorana **da** gidebiliriz. Benim için fark etmez.
  We can go to **either** restaurant. I don't mind.

- **(Her) iki** restoranı **da** beğenmedim.
  I didn't like **either** restaurant.

- Bu restoranlar**ın (her) ikisi de** çok iyi(dir).
  Both of these restaurants are very good.

- Restoranların **(her) ikisi de** pahalı **değil**.
  Neither of the restaurants is expensive.

- **(Her) ikimiz de** çok yorgunduk.
  Both of us were very tired.

(bizim) (her) ikimiz de	both of us
(sizin) (her) ikiniz de	both of you
(onların) (her) ikisi de	both of them

• NE.......... NE (DE) ...

The word '**ne**' has five principal uses:

1) As the interrogative for 'what?':

- **Ne** yaptın?   **What** did you do?
- **Ne** dedi?   **What** did he(she) say?

2)
- **Ne** güzel **bir** kız!   **What a** beautiful girl!
- **Ne** güzel!   **How** lovely!

3)
- **Ne** söylesem, doğrudur.
  Whatever I say is true.

4)
- **Ne** düşündüğün(üz), benim sorunum değil.
  What you think is not my problem.

5) ne...ne (de)...:
  ■ '**de**' is used to mean 'too, either or also'. It may be omitted.

- **Ne** Ali gördü, **ne (de)** Ayşe (gördü).
  Neither Ali **nor** Ayşe saw.

- **Ne** sen geldin, **ne (de)** onlar (geldiler).
  Neither you **nor** they came.

- **Ne** Aslı **ne de** Yılmaz, partiye gel**me**di.
- Partiye, **ne** Aslı geldi, **ne (de)** Yılmaz (geldi).
  Neither Aslı **nor** Yılmaz came to the party.

• HEM.....HEM DE... (BOTH....AND...)

- **Hem** Ali gördü, **hem (de)** Ayşe (gördü).
  Both Ali **and** Ayşe saw.

- **Hem** sen geldin, **hem (de)** ben (geldim)
  Both you **and** I came.

- Onlar **hem** yorgundular, **hem (de)** aç.
- Onlar **hem** yorgun, **hem (de)** açtılar.
  They were **both** tired **and** hungry.

- Film **hem** sıkıcı, **hem (de)** uzundu
- Film **hem** sıkıcıydı, **hem (de)** uzun.
  The film was **both** boring **and** long.

- **Hem** Aslı, **hem (de)** Okan geç kaldı(lar)
  Both Aslı **and** Okan were late.

• YA.... YA (DA) ...... (EITHER.....OR....)

◆ **'da'** is used to mean 'too'. It may be omitted.

- **Ya** Ali gördü, **ya (da)** Ayşe (gördü).
  Either Ali **or** Ayşe saw.

- **Ya** İspanyol(dur), **ya (da)** İtalyan(dır).
  He's **either** Spanish **or** Italian.

- Onlar, **ya** sinemaya gittiler, **ya (da)** tiyatroya (gittiler).
- Onlar, **ya** sinemaya, **ya (da)** tiyatroya gittiler.
  They went **either** to the cinema **or** to the theatre.

EXERCISE 45

Look at the following sentences and listen to the CD. Repeat the sentences in the gaps provided

1. Ne Orhan geldi, ne de Kayhan.
2. Ne Orhan gördü, ne de Kayhan gördü.
3. Hem Cem gitti, hem de Aslı.
4. Hem Ege geldi, hem Çağatay geldi.
5. Merve ve Pınar hem yorgundular, hem de aç.
6. Pervin ve Okan hem yorgun, hem de açtılar
7. Ya Orhan gördü, ya da Kayhan
8. Şu adam ya İspanyol dur, ya da İtalyan
9. Hiç İngiltere'de bulundunuz mu?
10. Hiç uçakla yolculuk ettiniz mi?
11. Fransa'da hiç bulunmadım.
12. Orada hiç kitap gördünüz mü?
13. Hiçbir şey görmedim.

KEY TO EXERCISES

EXERCISE 7-B)

1. Beş kilo şeker
2. Altmış gram
3. Altmış beş buçuk gram
4. Yarım kilo şeker
5. Üç yüz altmış beş gün
6. Elli iki hafta
7. On iki ay
8. Dokuz yüz doksan dokuz
9. On yıl
10. Ne kadar şeker?
11. Kaç tane elma?
12. Biraz süt
13. Birçok sandalye
14. Birkaç masa
15. Az su
16. Çok ağaç
17. Çok fazla öğrenci
18. Çok fazla et
19. Kaç tane portakal?
20. Çok az çay
21. Yedi kitap
22. Birkaç kitap
23. Çok para

EXERCISE 15

1. Ben bir şoför**üm**
2. Sen bir mühendis**sin**
3. O bir marangoz**dur**
4. Ben bir aşçı**yım**
5. Sen bir şoför**sün**
6. Sen bir mühendis**sin**
7. Sen bir marangoz**sun**
8. Sen bir aşçı**sın**
9. O bir aşçı**dır**
10. O bir şoför**dür**
11. O bir mühendis**tir**
12. O bir marangoz**dur**
13. O bir aşçı**dır**
14. Biz şoför**üz**
15. Biz mühendis**iz**
16. Biz marangoz**uz**
17. Biz aşçı**yız**
18. Siz şoför**sünüz**
19. Siz mühendis**siniz**
20. Siz marangoz**sunuz**
21. Siz aşçı**sınız**
22. Onlar şoför**dür(ler)**
23. Onlar mühendis**tir(ler)**
24. Onlar marangoz**dur(lar)**
25. Onlar aşçı**dır(lar)**
26. Ben bir şoför mü**yüm** ?
27. Sen bir mühendis mi**sin** ?
28. O bir marangoz mu**(dur)** ?
29. Biz aşçı mı**yız**?

EXERCISE 17

A)
1. Benim kalemim
2. Benim kitabım
3. Benim öğrencilerim
4. Senin masan
5. Senin gözlüğün
6. Onun televizyonu
7. Onun bardağı
8. Bizim dergimiz
9. Bizim kitabımız
10. Bizim sözlüğümüz
11. Sizin çatalınız
12. Sizin kaşığınız
13. Sizin kitaplarınız
14. Sizin sözlükleriniz
15. Onların kedisi
16. Onların köpeği

B)
1. Adamın saçı
2. Kadının eli
3. Okan'ın sözlüğü
4. Orçun'un kitabı
5. Benim kendi arabam
6. Senin (Sizin) kendi dergi(niz)
7. Bu araba benimki(dir)
8. O araba seninki(dir)
9. Onu tek başıma onardım

 ## EXERCISE 18

1. Bizim yeni bir arabamız var
2. Okan'ın (bir) baş ağrısı var
3. Hiç paran(ız) var mı ?
4. (Bir) ateşin(iz) var mı ?
5. Anahtarım yok
6. Orada bir ev var
7. Odada bir masa var
8. Evde (hiç) kimse yok
9. Bahçede iki kuzu var
10. Okulda hiç öğretmen yok

EXERCISE 19
A)
1.Ben dün erken uyandım - I woke up early yesterday
2.Sen yalnız mı gittin ? - Did you go alone ?
3.Ulaş dün işe geç kaldı - Ulaş was late for work yesterday
4.Okan ve Ben dün çok para harcadık - Okan and I spent a lot of money yesterday
5.Atakan ve sen filmi beğenmediniz - Atakan and you didn't enjoy the film
6.Okan ve Atakan partiden erken ayrıldılar - Okan and Atakan left the party early

B)
1. Aslı dün bir elbise satın aldı.
2. Dün akşam ne yaptın(ız) ?
3. Onu partiye çağırmadık (davet etmedik).
4. Pazartesi günü bana neden telefon etmedin ?
5. Onlar partiden saat onda ayrıldılar.

EXERCISE 21

1. Selin dün işteydi - Selin was at work yesterday
2. Neden sen o kadar kızgındın - Why were you so angry ?
3. Ben mühendistim - I was an engineer
4. Biz aç değildik - We were not hungry
5. Siz çok açtınız - You were very hungry
6. Onlar bana çok kızgındılar - They were very angry with me

EXERCISE 23

1. Ben kitabı Okan'a veriyorum
2. Sen çok iyi araba kullanıyorsun
3. Şafak Almanca öğreniyor.
4. Umut ve ben sigara içmiyoruz
5. Siz çok hızlı koşuyorsunuz.
6. Ulaş ve Buğra televizyondaki filme gülüyorlar.
7. Okan gülmüyor.
8. Sen kitabı kime veriyorsun?
9. Onlar nereye gidiyorlar?
10. Sen partiye geliyor musun?
11. Siz filmi izliyor musunuz?

EXERCISE 24

1. Ben çok iyi araba kullanıyordum.
2. Sen kitabı Ulaş'a veriyordun.
3. Tom sigara içmiyordu.

4. Umut ve ben Türkçe öğreniyorduk.
5. Siz televizyondaki filme gülüyordunuz.
6. Okan gülmüyordu.
7. Ulaş ve Buğra çok hızlı koşuyorlardı.
8. Ben hangi kitabı okuyordum ?
9. Siz nereye gidiyordunuz?
10. Onlar iyi Türkçe konuşuyorlar mıydı?
11. Aslı filmi izliyor muydu?

EXERCISE 25

1. Onu beş geçiyor
2. Dokuzu on geçiyor
3. Onu beş geçiyor
4. On biri çeyrek geçiyor
5. On bir buçuk
6. Üçe çeyrek var
7. Beşe yirmi beş var
8. Üçe beş var
9. Altıyı yirmi geçiyor

10. Beşe on var
11. Yedi buçuk
12. İkiyi yirmi altı geçiyor
13. Beşi on geçe
14. Altıyı yirmi geçe
15. İkiye yirmi kala
16. Dörde çeyrek kala
17. On buçukta

EXERCISE 27

1. Sık balığa giderim ve hiçbir şey yakalamam.
2. Et seversin(iz)
3. Ulaş araba alır ve satar.
4. Her gün pencerede otururuz ve trafiği izleriz
5. Sınıfta hiç uyur musun(uz)?
6. Kediler fare yakalar(lar).
7. Pencereyi açar mısın(ız) lütfen?
8. Gelir gelmez (or: varır varmaz) sana telefon ederim
9. Öğle yemeği için eve gelmem.
10. İşe arabayla gitmezler.

EXERCISE 28

1. (Ben) sık balığa **giderdim** ve hiçbir şey **yakalamazdım.**
2. (Sen) et **severdin.**
3. Ulaş araba **alır(dı)** ve **satardı.**
4. (Biz) her gün pencerede **oturur(duk)** ve trafiği **izlerdik.**
5. (Siz) hiç sınıfta **uyur muydunuz?**
6. (Ben) öğle yemeği için eve **gelmezdim.**
7. (Onlar) işe arabayla **gitmezlerdi.**

EXERCISE 29

1. Ben sizi orada **bekleyeceğim.**
   I will (am going to) wait for you there.
2. Sen gelecek yıl buraya **geleceksin.**
   You will (are going to) come here next year.
3. O evini **satacak.**
   He/She will (is going to) sell his house.
4. Biz nerede **kalacağız** ?
   Where will we stay? (where are we going to stay?)
5. Siz yarın evde **kalmayacaksınız.**
   You won't (aren't going to) stay at home tomorrow.
6. Onlar gelecek hafta yemek odasını **boyayacaklar.**
   They will (are going to) paint the dining room next week.
7. Biz sinemaya **gideceğiz.**
   We will (are going to) go to the cinema.

EXERCISE 30

1. (Onlar) partiye gitmişler.
2. Sen(Siz) o filmi görmüşsün(üz).
3. Bir araba satın almış.
4. Arabasını satmamış.
5. (Onlar) duvarı boyamamışlar.
6. (O) iyi koşarmış.
7. (Onlar) haftada beş kez sinemaya giderlermiş.
8. Sen(Siz) çok hızlı araba kullanırmışsın(ız).
9. (Onlar) Ankara'da yaşarlarmış (or: otururlarmış).

 ## EXERCISE 31

1.Film başladı mı / Film mi başladı ?
2.Aslı şu anda ne yapıyor? / Şu anda Aslı ne yapıyor?
3.Ne kadar sık dişçiye gidersin(iz)? / Dişçiye ne kadar sık gidersin(iz)?
4.Bisikletini onardı mı (tamir etti mi)? / Bisikletini mi onardı?
5.Ne zaman beni görmeye geleceksin(iz)? / Beni görmeye ne zaman geleceksin(iz)?
6.Neden arabalarını sattılar? / Arabalarını neden sattılar?
7.Onlar hangi kitabı okuyacaklardı / Hangi kitabı onlar okuyacaklardı ?

EXERCISE 32

1. Kitap, evden kaçan bir kız hakkında(dır).
2. Yarışı kazanan atın adı neydi?
3. Dolaptaki yumurtalar nerede(dir)?
4. Çok kibar olan bir (bayan) garson bize servis yaptı.
5. Bir sözlük, size sözcüklerin anlamını veren bir kitaptır.
6. Okan'ın 75 yaşındaki (or: 75 yaşında olan) babası, her gün yüzmeye gidiyor.

EXERCISE 33

1. Televizyonda maç izlerken, elektrik kesildi.
2. Ulaş'ı, ders çalışırken, hiç görmedim.
3. Araba kullanırken, çok dikkatli olun.
4. Hırsız, balkona tırmanırken, polise yakalandı.
5. Sandalda balık tutarken, fırtınaya yakalandık.

EXERCISE 34

1. Spor yapmak sağlığa yararlıdır.
2. Onun gitmesi iyi oldu.
3. Sizin kalmanız gerekiyor.
4. Senin okumanı tercih ederim.
5. Benim görmemi istiyor musunuz ?
6. Saat 6.00'da gitmeyi düşünüyorum.
7. Çalışmaya başladık
8. Televizyon izlemeye karar verdim.

 ## EXERCISE 35

1. Katı temizlemeyi bitirdim
2. Mektubu postalamayı unutma(yın)
3. Pencereyi açmayı unuttu.
4. Sigara içmeyi bırakacak mısın(ız) ?
       (or: Sigara içmeye son verecek misin(iz) ?)
5. Ulaş sinemaya gitmeyi önerdi.
6. O, Aslı'dan, ona biraz borç vermesini istedi
7. Sinemaya gitmeye karar verdik.
8. Yağmur yağmaya başladı.
9. Geç kalmamaya söz verdi.

EXERCISE 36

1.Ben trene bindiğim zaman, onu gördüm.
2.Sen Ankara'da olduğun yıl, hiç mektup yazmadın.
3.Onlar futbol maçına gittikleri (or: gittiği) gün, ben evdeydim.
4.Benim satın almayı istediğim araba çok pahalı.
5.Sizin okuduğunuz kitabı ben de okuyorum.
6.Senin böyle düşündüğüne inanmıyorum.
7.Sizin ne dediğinizi anlamıyorum.

EXERCISE 37

1. Şimdi git**meli**yim.
   I have to go now.
2. (Sen) Aslı'ya (mektup) yazma**lısın**.
   You have to write to Aslı.
3. (O) okumak için gözlük kullan**malı**.
   He/She has to wear glasses for reading.
3. (Biz) daha hızlı yürü**meliyiz**.
   We have to walk faster.
4. (Biz) hastaneye git**meli miyiz**?
   Do we have to go to hospital?
5. Dün (ben) erken kalk**malıydım**
   I had to get up early yesterday.
6. (Siz) partiden erken ayrılma**malıydınız**
   You shouldn't have left the party early.
7. (Biz) ne zaman ayrılmak zorunda**yız** ?
   When do we have to leave ?
8. (Siz) çalışmak zorunda**sınız**.
   You have to work.
9. (O) neden karakola gitmek zorunda**ydı**?
   Why did he have to go to the police station ?
10. Biz**im** erken ayrılma**mız** gerek**(iyor)** / gerek**li**.
    We have to (should) leave early.

EXERCISE 38

A)
1. Zili duyarsam, kapıya giderim (or: gideceğim) .
2. Yağmur durmazsa, dışarı gitmeyeceğiz (or: gitmeyiz)
3. Siz de gelseniz, çok iyi olur(du).
4. Köprü kırılsa, ne olur(du)?
5. Gitmeseydik, daha iyi olacaktı (or: olurdu).
6. Onu çağırsaydınız, gelecekti (or: gelirdi).

B)
1. If you wait, I'll come.
2. If I take a taxi I can catch the train.
3. If it rained, we would stay at home.
4. If they invited me, I would come.
5. If he had fallen into the river, he would have drowned.
6. If I hadn't heard some news, I wouldn't have written

EXERCISE 40
A)
1. Okan, "Rusça öğrenmek   istiyorum" dedi.
   Okan, Rusça öğrenmek istediğini söyledi.

2. Yıldız, "Dün Emre'yle yolda karşılaştım" dedi.
   Yıldız, dün Emre'yle yolda karşılaştığını söyledi.
3. Özben, "Damla sık dişçiye gider" dedi.
   Özben, Damla'nın sık dişçiye gittiğini söyledi.
4. Tolga, "Yarın bir iş görüşmesi yapacağım" dedi.
   Tolga, ertesi gün (or: yarın) bir iş görüşmesi yapacağını söyledi.
5. Atakan, Çetin'e "çok konuşmamalısın" dedi.
   Atakan, Çetin'e çok konuşmaması gerektiğini söyledi.

B)
1. Özlem, telefona yanıt vereceğini söyledi.
2. Okan Aslı'nın kendisine bir hediye verdiğini söyledi.
3. Onlar haberleri duymadıklarını söylediler
4. Ona, onu, piyanonun üstüne koymasını söyledim.
5. O, benden saçımı kestirmemi istedi.
6. Onlara, hemen ayrılmamız gerektiğini söyledik.
7. Ulaş, Özge'ye sorunun ne olduğunu sordu.
8. Emre, Şafak'a, Aslı'nın kalemi nereye koyduğunu sordu.
9. Onlar, telefonu kullanıp kullanamayacaklarını sordular.
10. Özlem, bana, bir ses duyup duymadığımı sordu.

 EXERCISE 41

A)
1. Temmuz'dan beri Rusça öğreniyorum.
2. İki saattir (iki saatten beri) koşuyoruz.
3. Altı aydır(altı aydan beri) iş arıyor.
4. Geçen yıldan beri sigara içiyorsun.

B)
1. İki saattir (iki saatten beri) okuyor
2. Saat ikiden beri çalışıyorum.
3. Ne kadar zamandır (Ne kadar zamandan beri) tenis oynuyorsunuz?
4. Onu beş saattir (beş saatten beri) bekliyoruz
5. Cumartesi'den beri (Cumartesi gününden beri) yağmur yağıyor.

 EXERCISE 42

1. Ben şimdi onları görebiliyorum
2. Sen şimdi onları görebiliyor musun?
3. Sonunda, Ulaş Buğra'yı yenebildi.
4. Yangın çabuk yayıldı fakat biz kaçabildik
5. Biz bu dağın zirvesine tırmanabiliriz
6. Siz uzun süre bekleyebilirsiniz
7. Okan, daha gençken, ağaca tırmanabilirdi(tırmanabiliyordu)
8. O, birkaç yıl önce, piyano çalabilirmiş (çalabiliyormuş)
9. Bu çorba, benim içemeyeceğim kadar sıcak
10. Hava, dışarı gidemeyeceğimiz kadar soğuk

EXERCISE 43

1. Dün, arabamı yıkattım.
2. Ayakkabılarımı her gün temizletirim
3. Okan,şu anda, saçını kestiriyor.
4. Fotoğrafımı çektireceğim.
5. Dün, ona, o ağacı kestirttim
6. Ona, arabayı boyattırdık

EXERCISE 44

A)
1. Köprü geçen yıl yapıldı.
   The bridge was built last year.
2. Pencere açılıyor.
   The window is being opened.
3. Sorunuz yanıtlanacak.
   Your question is going to be answered.
4. Bu resme her zaman hayran olunur.
   This picture is always admired.
5. Kitap gelecek ay bitirilecek.
   The book will be finished next month.

B)
1. Kız kardeşime de bir bilet verildi.
2. Bize, çeşitli sorular soruluyor.
3. Trenin ne zaman kalktığı, size söylenecek.
4. İş bitirilmeli.
5. O, yarın, hastaneye götürülecek.

INDEX

DISCOVER

TURKEY

at <u>www.asiaturkey.com</u>